GED® TEST SKILL BUILDER: LANGUAGE ARTS, READING

GED® TEST SKILL BUILDER: LANGUAGE ARTS, READING

LEARNINGEXPRESS®

NEW YORK

Library of Congress Cataloging-in-Publication Data:

GED® Test Skill Builder : language arts, reading.—First edition.
     pages   cm
  ISBN-13: 978-1-57685-795-3 (pbk. : alk. paper)
  ISBN-10: 1-57685-795-6 (pbk. : alk. paper)
 1. GED tests—Study guides.   2. Language arts (Secondary)—Examinations, questions, etc.—Study guides.
3. Reading (Secondary)—Examinations, questions, etc.—Study guides.
  LB3060.33.G45P65 2012
  373.126'2—dc23

2012008353

Printed in the United States of America

9 8 7 6 5 4 3 2 1

ISBN-13 978-157685-795-3

For more information or to place an order, contact LearningExpress at:
    2 Rector Street
    26th Floor
    New York, NY 10006

Or visit us at:
    www.learningexpressllc.com

Contents ▶

CONTENTS

INTRODUCTION

This book is designed to help people master the basic reading skills and concepts required to do well on the GED® Language Arts, Reading test. Many people who are preparing for this particular GED® test have not been in a school setting for some time. This means reading skills have gotten rusty or have been forgotten altogether. Others may have been in a school setting, but have not mastered various essential reading skills. By focusing on basic reading skills, this book will give its readers a better grasp of key reading concepts.

As the GED® Test Skill Builder title suggests, this book is not designed to prepare people to take the GED® test immediately afterward. Instead, its goal is to provide the necessary foundation of reading skills required for the GED® Language Arts, Reading test. Without these fundamental skills, it would be difficult for a person to prepare for the test effectively, much less earn a passable score. However, once these basic reading skills are understood, a person is then on the right path toward learning the concepts needed to succeed on this particular GED® test.

What This Book Contains

In addition to this introduction, GED® Test Skill Builder: Language Arts, Reading also contains the following:

- **The LearningExpress Test Preparation System.** Being a good test taker can boost anyone's GED® score. Many of the skills and strategies covered in this book will be familiar to anyone who has taken many multiple-choice tests, but there is a large difference between being "familiar with the strategy" and being "excellent at using the strategy." Our goal is to get you into that second category, and this chapter offers you the means to do so.
- **A Diagnostic Exam.** It's always helpful to see where your reading skills stand. Therefore, we recommend taking the diagnostic test before starting on the content chapters. By taking the diagnostic test, you should be able to determine the content areas in which you are strongest and the areas in which you might need more help. For example, if you miss most of your questions on the nonfiction passages, then you know that

you should pay extra attention when the book discusses the best ways to approach nonfiction passages.

The diagnostic test does not count for any score, so don't get caught up on how many you got right or wrong. Instead, use the results of the diagnostic test to help guide your study of the content chapters.

- **Content Chapters.** These chapters form the heart of the book. Here we cover the basic reading concepts discussed earlier. To help you understand all these ideas, every chapter has sample questions, helpful tips, summaries, as well as explanations of the concepts being discussed. We recommend reading these chapters in order and not skipping around, as many of the concepts in the earlier chapters are built on in the later chapters.
- **Two Practice Tests.** Once you have a better grasp of the basic reading skills, the best thing to do is to practice those skills. Both our practice tests are designed to be similar to the real GED® Language Arts, Reading test in terms of question types and passage content.

Taking these tests under timed conditions will help you gain familiarity with taking a timed reading test, which can help you in your GED® preparations. However, if you would prefer to work on the questions untimed in order to focus on mastering the basic concepts of the content chapters, that's not a bad idea, either. Either way is helpful preparation.

Preparing for any test takes time. While we understand that there are more enjoyable things to do than studying basic reading skills, the concepts contained in this book will be helpful to you not only during the GED® Language Arts, Reading test, but in your personal and professional life after the test as well.

Good luck, and good studying!

CHAPTER

THE LEARNINGEXPRESS TEST PREPARATION SYSTEM

Taking any written exam can be tough. It demands a lot of preparation if you want to achieve the best possible score. The LearningExpress Test Preparation System, developed exclusively for LearningExpress by leading test experts, gives you the discipline and attitude you need to be a winner.

Taking the GED® Language Arts, Reading test is no picnic, and neither is getting ready for it. You want to earn the highest possible score, but there are all sorts of pitfalls that can keep you from doing your best on this all-important exam. Here are some of the obstacles that can stand in the way of your success:

- being unfamiliar with the format of the exam
- being paralyzed by test anxiety
- leaving your preparation until the last minute or not preparing at all
- not knowing vital test-taking skills: how to pace yourself through the exam, how to use the process of elimination, and when to guess

- not being in tip-top mental and physical shape
- messing up on exam day by having to work on an empty stomach or shivering through the exam because the room is cold

What's the common denominator in all these test-taking pitfalls? One word: *control*. Who's in control, you or the exam? The LearningExpress Test Preparation System puts you in control. In just nine easy-to-follow steps, you will learn everything you need to know to make sure that you are in charge of your preparation and your performance on this GED® test. Other test takers may let the exam get the better of them; other test takers may be unprepared or out of shape, but not you. After completing this chapter, you will have taken all the steps you need to get a high score on the GED® Language Arts, Reading test.

Here's how the LearningExpress Test Preparation System works: nine easy steps lead you through everything you need to know and do to get ready for this exam. Each of the steps listed here and discussed in detail on the following pages includes both reading about the step and one or more activities. It's important that you do the activities along with the reading, or you won't be getting the full benefit of the system. Each step tells you approximately how much time that step will take you to complete.

Step 1: Get Information (30 minutes)
Step 2: Conquer Test Anxiety (20 minutes)
Step 3: Make a Plan (50 minutes)
Step 4: Learn to Manage Your Time (10 minutes)
Step 5: Learn to Use the Process of Elimination (20 minutes)
Step 6: Know When to Guess (20 minutes)
Step 7: Reach Your Peak Performance Zone (10 minutes)
Step 8: Get Your Act Together (10 minutes)

Step 9: Do It! (10 minutes)
Total time for complete system: (180 minutes— 3 hours)

We estimate that working through the entire system will take you approximately three hours. It's perfectly okay if you work at a faster or slower pace. If you can take a whole afternoon or evening, you can work through the whole LearningExpress Test Preparation System in one sitting. Otherwise, you can break it up and do just one or two steps a day for the next several days. It's up to you—remember, you are in control.

Step 1: Get Information

Time to complete: 30 minutes
Activity: Read the Introduction to This Book
Knowledge is power. The first step in the LearningExpress Test Preparation System is finding out everything you can about the types of information you will be expected to know and how this knowledge will be assessed.

What You Should Find Out
The more details you can find out about the exam, the more efficiently you will be able to study. Here's a list of some things you might want to find out:

- What skills are tested?
- How many sections are on the exam?
- How many questions are in each section?
- How much time is allotted for each section?
- How is the exam scored, and is there a penalty for wrong answers?
- Can you write in the exam booklet, or will you be given scratch paper?

Step 2: Conquer Test Anxiety

Time to complete: 20 minutes
Activity: Take the *Test Anxiety Quiz* (later in this chapter)

Having complete information about the GED® Language Arts, Reading test is the first step in getting control of it. Next, you have to overcome one of the biggest obstacles to test success: *test anxiety*. Test anxiety can not only impair your performance on the exam itself, but it can even keep you from preparing properly. In Step 2, you will learn stress management techniques that will help you succeed on your exam. Learn these strategies now, and practice them as you work through the activities in this book so that they'll be second nature to you by exam day.

Combating Test Anxiety

The first thing you need to know is that a little test anxiety is a good thing. Everyone gets nervous before a big exam—and if that nervousness motivates you to prepare thoroughly, so much the better. It's said that Sir Laurence Olivier, one of the foremost British actors of the twentieth century, threw up before every performance. His stage fright didn't impair his performance; in fact, it probably gave him a little extra edge—just the kind of edge you need to do well, whether on a stage or in an examination room. At the end of this section is the *Test Anxiety Quiz*. Stop here and answer the questions on that page to find out whether your level of test anxiety is something you should worry about.

Stress Management before the Exam

If you feel your level of anxiety is getting the best of you in the weeks before the exam, here is what you need to do to bring that level down again:

- **Get prepared.** There's nothing like knowing what to expect and being prepared for it to put you in control of test anxiety. That's why you're reading this book. Use it faithfully, and remind yourself that you're better prepared than most of the people taking the exam.
- **Practice self-confidence.** A positive attitude is a great way to combat test anxiety. This is no time to be humble or shy. Stand in front of the mirror and say to your reflection, "I'm prepared. I'm full of self-confidence. I'm going to ace this exam. I know I can do it." Say it into a recorder and play it back once a day. If you hear it often enough, you will believe it.
- **Fight negative messages.** Every time someone starts telling you how hard the exam is or how difficult it is to get a high score, start reciting your self-confidence messages to that person. If the someone with the negative messages is you—telling yourself you don't do well on exams, that you just can't do this—don't listen. Turn on your recorder and listen to your self-confidence messages.
- **Visualize.** Imagine yourself sitting in your first day of college classes or beginning the first day of your dream job because you have earned your GED® credentials. Visualizing success can help make it happen—and it reminds you of why you're doing all this work in preparing for the exam.
- **Exercise.** Physical activity helps calm down your body and focus your mind. Besides, being in good physical shape can actually help you do well on the exam. Go for a run, lift weights, go swimming—and do it regularly.

Stress Management on Test Day

There are several ways you can bring down your level of test stress and anxiety on test day. They'll work best if you practice them in the weeks before the exam, so you know which ones work best for you.

- **Deep breathing.** Take a deep breath while you count to five, hold it for a count of one, and then let it out on a count of five. Repeat several times.

You need to worry about test anxiety only if it is extreme enough to impair your performance. The following questionnaire will provide a diagnosis of your level of test anxiety. In the blank before each statement, write the number that most accurately describes your experience.

0 = Never
1 = Once or twice
2 = Sometimes
3 = Often

_____ I have gotten so nervous before an exam that I simply put down the books and didn't study for it.

_____ I have experienced disabling physical symptoms such as vomiting and severe headaches because I was nervous about an exam.

_____ I have simply not showed up for an exam because I was afraid to take it.

_____ I have experienced dizziness and disorientation while taking an exam.

_____ I have had trouble filling in the little circles because my hands were shaking too hard.

_____ I have failed an exam because I was too nervous to complete it.

_____ **Total: Add up the numbers in the blanks.**

Understanding Your Test Stress Score

Here are the steps you should take, depending on your score. If you scored

- **Below 3:** Your level of test anxiety is nothing to worry about; it's probably just enough to give you that little extra edge.

- **Between 3 and 6:** Your test anxiety may be enough to impair your performance, and you should practice the stress management techniques in this section to try to bring your test anxiety down to manageable levels.

- **Above 6:** Your level of test anxiety is a serious concern. In addition to practicing the stress management techniques listed in this section, you may want to seek additional personal help. Call your local high school or community college and ask for the academic counselor. Tell the counselor that you have a level of test anxiety that sometimes keeps you from being able to take an exam. The counselor may be willing to help you or may suggest someone else you should talk to.

- **Move your body**. Try rolling your head in a circle. Rotate your shoulders. Shake your hands from the wrist. Many people find these movements very relaxing.
- **Visualize again.** Think of the place where you are most relaxed: lying on the beach in the sun, walking through the park, or whatever relaxes you. Now, close your eyes and imagine you're actually there. If you practice in advance, you will find that you need only a few seconds of this exercise to experience a significant increase in your sense of well-being.

When anxiety threatens to overwhelm you *during* the test, there are still things you can do to manage your stress level:

- **Repeat your self-confidence messages.** You should have them memorized by now. Say them quietly to yourself, and believe them!
- **Visualize one more time.** This time, visualize yourself moving smoothly and quickly through the exam, answering every question correctly, and finishing just before time is up. Like most visualization techniques, this one works best if you've practiced it ahead of time.
- **Find an easy question.** Skim over the questions on Part I until you find an easy question, and answer it. Getting even one question answered correctly gets you into the test-taking groove.
- **Take a mental break.** Everyone loses concentration once in a while during a long exam. It's normal, so you shouldn't worry about it. Instead, accept what has happened. Say to yourself, "Hey, I lost it there for a minute. My brain is taking a break." Put down your pencil, close your eyes, and do some deep breathing for a few seconds. Then, you're ready to go back to work.

Try these techniques ahead of time, and see whether they work for you!

Step 3: Make a Plan

Time to complete: 50 minutes
Activity: Construct a Study Plan, using Schedules A through D (later in this section)

Many people do poorly on exams because they forget to make a study schedule. The most important thing you can do to better prepare yourself for your exam is to create a study plan or schedule. Spending hours the day before the exam poring over sample test questions not only raises your level of anxiety, but it also does not substitute for careful preparation and practice over time.

Don't cram. Take control of your time by mapping out a study schedule. There are four examples of study schedules on the following pages, based on the amount of time you have before the exam. If you're the kind of person who needs deadlines and assignments to motivate you for a project, here they are. If you're the kind of person who doesn't like to follow other people's plans, you can use the suggested schedules to construct your own.

In constructing your plan, take into account how much work you need to do. If your score on the diagnostic test in this book isn't what you had hoped, consider taking some of the steps from Schedule A and fitting them into Schedule D, even if you do have only three weeks before the exam. (See Schedules A through D on the next few pages.)

Even more important than making a plan is making a commitment. You can't review everything you've learned in middle or high school in one night. You have to set aside some time every day for studying and practice. Try to set aside at least 20 minutes a day. Twenty minutes daily will do you more good than two hours crammed into a Saturday. If you have months before the test, you're lucky. Don't put off your studying until the week before. Start now. Even ten minutes a day, with half an hour or more on weekends, can make a big difference in your score.

Schedule A: The Leisure Plan

This schedule gives you at least six months to sharpen your skills and prepare for the GED® Language Arts, Reading test. The more prep time you give yourself, the more relaxed you'll feel.

- **Test day minus 6 months:** Take the diagnostic test in Chapter 2, then review the correct answers and the explanations. Start going to the library once every two weeks to read books or information about successful reading strategies. Find other people who are preparing for the exam and form a study group.
- **Test day minus 5 months:** Read Chapters 3 and 4 and work through the exercises. Use at least one of the additional resources for each chapter as you read it.
- **Test day minus 4 months:** Read Chapter 5 and work through the exercises. You're still continuing with your reading, aren't you?
- **Test day minus 3 months:** Read Chapter 6 and work through the exercises.
- **Test day minus 2 months:** Use your scores from the chapter exercises to help you decide where to concentrate your efforts this month. Go back to the relevant chapters and reread the information. Continue working with your study group.
- **Test day minus 1 month:** Read Chapter 7. Then, review the end-of-chapter quizzes and chapter review boxes in Chapters 3 through 6.
- **Test day minus 1 week:** Take and review the sample exams in Chapters 8 and 9. See how much you've learned in the past months. Concentrate on what you've done well and decide not to let any areas where you still feel uncertain bother you.
- **Day before test:** Relax. Do something unrelated to the GED® test. Eat a good meal and go to bed at your usual time.

Schedule B: The Just-Enough-Time Plan

If you have three to six months before the test, that should be enough time to prepare. This schedule assumes four months; stretch it out or compress it if you have more or less time.

- **Test day minus 4 months:** Take the diagnostic test in Chapter 2 and review the correct answers and the explanations. Then read Chapter 3 and work through the exercises. Start going to the library once every two weeks to read books or information about successful reading strategies.
- **Test day minus 3 months:** Read Chapters 4 and 5 and work through the exercises.
- **Test day minus 2 months:** Read Chapter 6 and work through the exercises. You're still continuing with your reading, aren't you?
- **Test day minus 1 month:** Take one of the sample exams in either Chapter 8 or 9. Use your score to help you decide where to concentrate your efforts this month. Go back to the relevant chapters and reread the information or get the help of a friend or teacher.
- **Test day minus 1 week:** Review Chapter 7 one last time and take the other sample exam. See how much you've learned in the past months. Concentrate on what you've done well and decide not to let any areas where you still feel uncertain bother you.
- **Day before test:** Relax. Do something unrelated to the GED® test. Eat a good meal and go to bed at your usual time.

Schedule C: More Study in Less Time

If you have one to three months before the test, you still have enough time for some concentrated study that will help you improve your score. This schedule is built around a two-month time frame. If you have only one month, spend an extra couple of hours a week to get all these steps in. If you have three months, take some of the steps from Schedule B and fit them in.

- **Test day minus 8 weeks:** Take the diagnostic test in Chapter 2 and review the correct answers and the explanations. Then read Chapter 3. Work through the exercises in these chapters. Review the areas you're weakest in.
- **Test day minus 6 weeks:** Read Chapters 4 and 5 and work through the exercises.
- **Test day minus 4 weeks:** Read Chapters 6 and 7 and work through the exercises.
- **Test day minus 2 weeks:** Take one of the practice exams in Chapter 8 or 9. Then, score it and read the answer explanations until you're sure you understand them. Review the areas where your score is lowest.
- **Test day minus 1 week:** Take the other sample exam. Then review both exams, concentrating on the areas where a little work can help the most.
- **Day before test:** Relax. Do something unrelated to the GED. Eat a good meal and go to bed at your usual time.

Schedule D: The Cram Plan

If you have three weeks or less before the test, you really have your work cut out for you. Carve half an hour out of your day, every day, for studying. This schedule assumes you have the whole three weeks to prepare; if you have less time, you will have to compress the schedule accordingly.

- **Test day minus 3 weeks:** Take the diagnostic test in Chapter 2 and review the correct answers and the explanations. Then read Chapters 3 and 4. Work through the exercises in the chapters. Review areas you're weakest in.
- **Test day minus 2 weeks:** Read the material in chapters 5 through 7 and work through the exercises.
- **Test day minus 1 week:** Evaluate your performance on the chapter quizzes. Review the parts of chapters that explain the skills you had the most trouble with. Get a friend or teacher to help you with the section you had the most difficulty with.

- **Test day minus 2 days:** Take the sample exams in Chapters 8 and 9. Review your results. Make sure you understand the answer explanations. Review the sample essay outline in Chapter 5 and reread the end of the chapter review box.
- **Day before test:** Relax. Do something unrelated to the GED® test. Eat a good meal and go to bed at your usual time.

Step 4: Learn to Manage Your Time

Time to complete: 10 minutes to read, many hours of practice

Activities: Practice these strategies as you take the sample exams

Steps 4, 5, and 6 of the LearningExpress Test Preparation System put you in charge of your GED test by showing you test-taking strategies that work. Practice these strategies as you take the diagnostic test, sample quizzes, and practice exams throughout this book. Then, you will be ready to use them on test day.

First, you will take control of your time on the GED® test. The first step in achieving this control is to understand the format of the test. The GED Language Arts, Reading exam includes 40 multiple-choice questions and allows 65 minutes. You will want to practice using your time wisely on the practice tests and chapter quizzes and trying to avoid mistakes while working quickly.

- **Listen carefully to directions.** By the time you get to the test, you should know how the test works, but listen just in case something has changed.
- **Pace yourself.** Glance at your watch every few minutes and compare the time to how far you've gotten in the section. Leave some extra time for review so that when one quarter of the time has elapsed, you should be more than a quarter of the way through the section, and so on. If you're falling behind, pick up the pace.

- **Keep moving.** Don't spend too much time on one question. If you don't know the answer, skip the question and move on. Circle the number of the question in your test booklet in case you have time to come back to it later.
- **Keep track of your place on the answer sheet.** If you skip a question, make sure you skip on the answer sheet, too. Check yourself every five to ten questions to make sure the question number and the answer sheet number match.
- **Don't rush.** You should keep moving, but rushing won't help. Try to keep calm and work methodically and quickly.

Step 5: Learn to Use the Process of Elimination

Time to complete: 20 minutes
Activity: Complete *Using the Process of Elimination* worksheet (later in this section)

After time management, the next most important tool for taking control of your test is using the process of elimination wisely. It's standard test-taking wisdom that you should always read all the answer choices before choosing your answer. This helps you find the right answer by eliminating wrong answer choices. And, sure enough, that standard wisdom applies to this exam, too. Let's say you're facing a question that goes like this:

9. Sentence 6: I would like to be considered for the assistant manager position in your company my previous work experience is a good match for the job requirements posted.

Which correction should be made to sentence 6?
a. Insert *Although* before *I.*
b. Insert a question mark after *company.*
c. Insert a semicolon and *however* before *my.*
d. Insert a period after *company* and capitalize *my.*
e. No corrections are necessary.

If you happen to know that sentence 6 is a run-on sentence, and you know how to correct it, you don't need to use the process of elimination. But let's assume that, like some people, you don't. So, you look at the answer choices. *Although* sure doesn't sound like a good choice because it would change the meaning of the sentence. So, you eliminate choice **a**—and now you only have four answer choices to deal with. Mark an **X** next to choice **a**, so you never have to read it again. Move on to the other answer choices. If you know that the first part of the sentence does not ask a question, you can eliminate answer **b** as a possible answer. Make an **X** beside it. Choice **c**, inserting a semicolon, could create a pause in an otherwise long sentence, but inserting the word *however* might not be correct. If you're not sure whether or not this answer is correct, put a question mark beside it, meaning, "Well, maybe." Answer choice **d** would separate a very long sentence into two shorter sentences and would not change the meaning. It could work, so put a check mark beside it meaning "Good answer. I might use this one." Answer choice **e** means that the sentence is fine as it is and doesn't need any changes. The sentence could make sense as it is, but it is definitely long. Is this the best way to write the sentence? If you're not sure, put a question mark beside answer choice **e.**

Now, your question looks like this:

Which correction should be made to sentence 6?
X **a.** Insert *Although* before *I.*
X **b.** Insert a question mark after *company.*
? **c.** Insert a semicolon and *however* before *my.*
✓ **d.** Insert a period after *company* and capitalize *my.*
? **e.** No corrections are necessary.

You've got just one check mark, signifying a *good answer*. If you're pressed for time, you should simply mark answer **d** on your answer sheet. If you've got the time to be extra careful, you could compare your check mark answer to your question mark answers to make sure that it's better. (It is. Sentence 6 is a run-on sentence and should be separated into two shorter, complete sentences.)

It's good to have a system for marking *good*, *bad*, and *maybe* answers. We recommend using this one:

X = bad
✓ = good
? = maybe

If you don't like these marks, devise your own system. Just make sure you do it long before exam day—while you're working through the practice tests and quizzes in this book—so you won't have to worry about it during the exam.

Even when you think you're absolutely clueless about a question, you can often use the process of elimination to get rid of one answer choice. If so, you're better prepared to make an educated guess, as you will see in Step 6. More often, the process of elimination allows you to get down to only two possibly right answers. Then, you're in a strong position to guess. And sometimes, even though you don't know the right answer, you find it simply by getting rid of the wrong ones, as you did in the previous example.

Try answering the questions on the *Using the Process of Elimination* worksheet. The answer explanations show one possible way you might use the process to arrive at the right answer. The process of elimination is your tool for the next step, which is knowing when to guess.

Step 6: Know When to Guess

Time to complete: 20 minutes
Activity: Complete *Your Guessing Ability*
worksheet

Armed with the process of elimination, you're ready to take control of one of the big questions in test taking: *Should I guess?* The first and main answer is *yes*. Unless the exam has a so-called guessing penalty, you have

nothing to lose and everything to gain from guessing. The more complicated answer depends both on the exam and on you—your personality and your *guessing intuition.*

The GED® Language Arts, Reading test doesn't use a guessing penalty. The multiple choice questions you answer correctly on Part I earn one point each, and you simply do not earn a point for wrong answers. So most of the time, you don't have to worry—simply go ahead and guess. But if you find that a test does have a guessing penalty, you should read the next section to find out what that means for you.

How the Guessing Penalty Works

A guessing penalty really only works against random guessing—filling in the little circles to make a nice pattern on your answer sheet. If you can eliminate one or more answer choices, as just outlined, you're better off taking a guess than leaving the answer blank, even on the sections that have a penalty.

Here's how a guessing penalty works: Depending on the number of answer choices in a given exam, some proportion of the number of questions you get wrong is subtracted from the total number of questions you got right. For instance, if there are four answer choices, typically the guessing penalty is one-third of your wrong answers. Suppose you took an exam of 100 questions. You answered 88 of them right and 12 wrong. If there's no guessing penalty, your score is simply 88. But if there's a one-third point guessing penalty, the scorers take your 12 wrong answers and divide by three to come up with four. Then, they subtract that four from your correct answer score of 88 to leave you with a score of 84. Thus, you would have been better off if you had simply not answered those 12 questions. Then, your total score would still be 88 because there wouldn't be anything to subtract.

What You Should Do about the Guessing Penalty

You now know how a guessing penalty works. The first thing this means for you is that marking your answer

Use the process of elimination to answer the following questions.

1. Ilsa is as old as Meghan will be in five years. The difference between Ed's age and Meghan's age is twice the difference between Ilsa's age and Meghan's age. Ed is 29. How old is Ilsa?
   a. 4
   b. 10
   c. 19
   d. 24

2. "All drivers of commercial vehicles must carry a valid commercial driver's license whenever operating a commercial vehicle."

   According to this sentence, which of the following people need NOT carry a commercial driver's license?
   a. a truck driver idling his engine while waiting to be directed to a loading dock
   b. a bus operator backing her bus out of the way of another bus in the bus lot
   c. a taxi driver driving his personal car to the grocery store
   d. a limousine driver taking the limousine to her home after dropping off her last passenger of the evening

3. Smoking tobacco has been linked to
   a. increased risk of stroke and heart attack.
   b. all forms of respiratory disease.
   c. increasing mortality rates over the past ten years.
   d. juvenile delinquency.

4. Which of the following words is spelled correctly?
   a. incorrigible
   b. outragous
   c. domestickated
   d. understandible

Answers

Here are the answers as well as some suggestions as to how you might have used the process of elimination to find them.

1. d. You should have eliminated choice **a** right off the bat. Ilsa can't be four years old if Meghan is going to be Ilsa's age in five years. The best way to eliminate other answer choices is to try plugging them into the information given in the problem. For instance, for choice **b**, if Ilsa is 10, then Meghan must be 5. The difference between their ages is 5. The difference between Ed's age, 29, and Meghan's age, 5, is 24. Is 24 two times 5? No. Then choice **b** is wrong. You could eliminate choice **c** in the same way and be left with choice **d**.

2. c. Note the word not in the question and go through the answers one by one. Is the truck driver in choice **a** "operating a commercial vehicle"? Yes, idling counts as "operating," so he needs to have a commercial driver's license. Likewise, the bus operator in choice **b** is operating a commercial vehicle; the question doesn't say the operator has to be on the street. The limo driver in choice **d** is operating

a commercial vehicle, even though it doesn't have a passenger in it. However, the driver in choice **c** is not operating a commercial vehicle but his own private car.

3. a. You could eliminate choice **b** simply because of the presence of the word *all*. Such absolutes hardly ever appear in correct answer choices. Choice **c** looks attractive until you think a little about what you know—aren't fewer people smoking these days, rather than more? So how could smoking be responsible for a higher mortality rate? (If you didn't know that mortality rate means the rate at which people die, you might keep this choice as a possibility, but you would still be able to eliminate two answers and have only two to choose from.) And choice **d** is plain silly, so you could eliminate that one, too. You are left with the correct choice, **a**.

4. a. How you used the process of elimination here depends on which words you recognized as being spelled incorrectly. If you knew that the correct spellings were *outrageous*, *domesticated*, and *understandable*, then you were home free. Surely you knew that at least one of these words was wrong!

Your Guessing Ability

The following are ten really hard questions. You are not supposed to know the answers. Rather, this is an assessment of your ability to guess when you don't have a clue. Read each question carefully, as if you were expected to answer it. If you have any knowledge of the subject, use that knowledge to help you eliminate wrong answer choices.

1. September 7 is Independence Day in
   a. India.
   b. Costa Rica.
   c. Brazil.
   d. Australia.

2. Which of the following is the formula for determining the momentum of an object?
   a. $p = mv$
   b. $F = ma$
   c. $P = IV$
   d. $E = mc^2$

3. Because of the expansion of the universe, the stars and other celestial bodies are all moving away from one another. This phenomenon is known as
   a. Newton's first law.
   b. the big bang.
   c. gravitational collapse.
   d. Hubble flow.

4. American author Gertrude Stein was born in
   a. 1713.
   b. 1830.
   c. 1874.
   d. 1901.

5. Which of the following is NOT one of the Five Classics attributed to Confucius?
   a. *I Ching*
   b. *Book of Holiness*
   c. *Spring and Autumn Annals*
   d. *Book of History*

6. The religious and philosophical doctrine that holds that the universe is constantly in a struggle between good and evil is known as
   a. Pelagianism.
   b. Manichaeanism.
   c. neo-Hegelianism.
   d. Epicureanism.

7. The third Chief Justice of the U.S. Supreme Court was
   a. John Blair.
   b. William Cushing.
   c. James Wilson.
   d. John Jay.

8. Which of the following is the poisonous portion of a daffodil?
   a. the bulb
   b. the leaves
   c. the stem
   d. the flowers

9. The winner of the Masters golf tournament in 1953 was
   a. Sam Snead.
   b. Cary Middlecoff.
   c. Arnold Palmer.
   d. Ben Hogan.

10. The state with the highest per capita personal income in 1980 was
   a. Alaska.
   b. Connecticut.
   c. New York.
   d. Texas.

Answers

Check your answers against the following correct answers.

1. c.
2. a.
3. d.
4. c.
5. b.
6. b.
7. b.
8. a.
9. d.
10. a.

How Did You Do?

You may have simply gotten lucky and actually known the answer to one or two questions. In addition, your guessing was probably more successful if you were able to use the process of elimination on any of the questions. Maybe you didn't know who the third Chief Justice was (question 7), but you knew that John Jay was the first. In that case, you would have eliminated choice **d** and, therefore, improved your odds of guessing right from one in four to one in three.

According to probability, you should get two-and-a-half answers correct, so getting either two or three right would be average. If you got four or more right, you may be a really terrific guesser. If you got one or none right, you may be a really bad guesser.

Keep in mind, though, that this is only a small sample. You should continue to keep track of your guessing ability as you work through the sample test questions in this book. Circle the numbers of questions you guess on as you make your guess; or, if you don't have time while you take the practice tests, go back afterward and try to remember which questions you guessed at.

Remember, on a test with four answer choices, your chance of guessing correctly is one in four. On a test such as the GED® test, which has five answer choices, your chance of getting a right answer is one in five. So keep a separate "guessing" score for each exam. How many questions did you guess on? How many did you get right? If the number you got right is at least one-fourth of the number of questions you guessed on, you are at least an average guesser—maybe better—and you should always go ahead and guess on the real exam. If the number you got right is significantly lower than one-fourth of the number you guessed on, you would be safe in guessing anyway, but maybe you would feel more comfortable if you guessed only selectively, when you can eliminate a wrong answer or at least have a good feeling about one of the answer choices.

Remember, even if you are a play-it-safe person with lousy intuition, you are still safe guessing every time.

sheet at random doesn't pay off. If you're running out of time on an exam that has a guessing penalty, you should not use your remaining seconds to mark a pretty pattern on your answer sheet. Take those few seconds to try to answer one more question right. But as soon as you get out of the realm of random guessing, the guessing penalty no longer works against you. If you can use the process of elimination to get rid of even one wrong answer choice, the odds stop being against you and start working in your favor.

Sticking with our example of an exam that has four answer choices, eliminating just one wrong answer makes your odds of choosing the correct answer one in three. That's the same as the one-out-of-three guessing penalty—even odds. If you eliminate two answer choices, your odds are one in two—better than the guessing penalty. In either case, you should go ahead and choose one of the remaining answer choices.

When There Is No Guessing Penalty

As previously noted, the GED Language Arts, Reading exam does *not* have a guessing penalty. That means that, all other things being equal, you should always go ahead and guess, even if you have no idea what the question means. Nothing can happen to you if you're wrong. But all other things aren't necessarily equal. The other factor in deciding whether to guess, besides the guessing penalty, is you. There are two things you need to know about yourself before you go into the exam:

- Are you a risk-taker?
- Are you a good guesser?

Your risk-taking temperament matters most on exams with a guessing penalty. Without a guessing penalty, even if you're a play-it-safe person, guessing is perfectly safe. Overcome your anxieties and go ahead

and mark an answer. But what if you're not much of a risk taker, and you think of yourself as the world's worst guesser? Complete the *Your Guessing Ability* worksheet to get an idea of how good your intuition is.

Step 7: Reach Your Peak Performance Zone

Time to complete: 10 minutes to read; weeks to complete!
Activity: Complete the *Physical Preparation Checklist*

To get ready for a challenge like a big test, you have to take control of your physical, as well as your mental, state. Exercise, proper diet, and rest will ensure that your body works with, rather than against, your mind on test day as well as during your preparation.

Exercise

If you don't already have a regular exercise program going, the time during which you're preparing for an exam is actually an excellent time to start one. And if you're already keeping fit—or trying to get that way—don't let the pressure of preparing for an exam fool you into quitting now. Exercise helps reduce stress by pumping wonderful, good-feeling hormones called *endorphins* into your system. It also increases the oxygen supply throughout your body, including your brain, so you will be at peak performance on exam day.

A half hour of vigorous activity—enough to raise a sweat—every day should be your aim. If you're really pressed for time, every other day is okay. Choose an activity you like and get out there and do it. Jogging with a friend always makes the time go faster, as does running with a MP3 player. But don't overdo it. You don't want to exhaust yourself. Moderation is the key.

For the week before the test, write down what physical exercise you engaged in and for how long and what you ate for each meal. Remember, you're trying for at least half an hour of exercise every other day (preferably every day) and a balanced diet that's light on junk food.

Exam day minus 7 days

Exercise: _____ for _____ minutes

Breakfast: _____

Lunch: _____

Dinner: _____

Snacks: _____

Exam day minus 6 days

Exercise: _____ for _____ minutes

Breakfast: _____

Lunch: _____

Dinner: _____

Snacks: _____

Exam day minus 5 days

Exercise: _____ for _____ minutes

Breakfast: _____

Lunch: _____

Dinner: _____

Snacks: _____

Exam day minus 4 days

Exercise: _____ for _____ minutes

Breakfast: _____

Lunch: _____

Dinner: _____

Snacks: _____

Exam day minus 3 days

Exercise: _____ for _____ minutes

Breakfast: _____

Lunch: _____

Dinner: _____

Snacks: _____

Exam day minus 2 days

Exercise: _____ for _____ minutes

Breakfast: _____

Lunch: _____

Dinner: _____

Snacks: _____

Day before exam

Exercise: _____ for _____ minutes

Breakfast: _____

Lunch: _____

Dinner: _____

Snacks: _____

Diet

First of all, cut out the junk. Then, go easy on caffeine. What your body needs for peak performance is simply a balanced diet. Eat plenty of fruits and vegetables, along with protein and carbohydrates. Foods that are high in lecithin (an amino acid), such as fish and beans, are especially good brain foods. The night before the test, you might carbo-load the way athletes do before a contest. Eat a big plate of spaghetti, rice and beans, or whatever your favorite carbohydrate is.

Rest

You probably know how much sleep you need every night to be at your best, even if you don't always get it. Make sure you do get that much sleep, though, for at least a week before the exam. Moderation is important here, too. Too much sleep will just make you groggy.

If you are not a morning person and your test will be given in the morning, you should reset your internal clock so that your body doesn't think you're taking an exam at 3 a.m. You have to start this process well before the day of the test. The way it works is to get up half an hour earlier each morning and then go to bed half an hour earlier each night. Don't try it the other way around; you will just toss and turn if you go to bed early without having gotten up early. The next morning, get up another half an hour earlier, and so on. How long you will have to do this depends on how late you're used to getting up. Use the *Physical Preparation Checklist* to make sure you're in tip-top form.

Step 8: Get Your Act Together

Time to complete: 10 minutes to read; time to complete will vary
Activity: Complete *Final Preparations* worksheet
You're in control of your mind and body; you're in charge of test anxiety, your preparation, and your test-taking strategies. Now, it's time to take charge of external factors, like the testing site and the materials you need to take the exam.

Find Out Where the Exam Is and Make a Trial Run

Make sure you know exactly when and where your test is being held. Do you know how to get to the exam site? Do you know how long it will take to get there? If not, make a trial run, preferably on the same day of the week at the same time of day as the real test. Note on the *Final Preparations* worksheet the amount of time it will take you to get to the test site. Plan on arriving 10 to 15 minutes early so that you can get the lay of the land, use the bathroom, and calm down. Then, figure out how early you will have to get up that morning and make sure you get up that early every day for a week before the test.

Gather Your Materials

The night before the exam, lay out the clothes you will wear and the materials you have to bring with you to the test. Plan on dressing in layers; you won't have any control over the temperature of the examination room. Have a sweater or jacket you can take off if it's warm. Use the checklist on the *Final Preparations* worksheet to help you pull together what you will need.

Don't Skip Breakfast

Even if you don't usually eat breakfast, do so on the morning of the test. A cup of coffee or can of soda doesn't count. Don't eat doughnuts or other sweet foods, either. A sugar high will leave you with a sugar low in the middle of the test. A mix of protein and carbohydrates is best. Cereal with milk and just a little sugar or eggs with toast will do your body a world of good.

Step 9: Do It!

Time to complete: 10 minutes, plus test-taking time
Activity: Ace the GED® Language Arts, Reading
       Test!

Fast-forward to test day. You're ready. You made a study plan and followed through. You practiced your test-taking strategies while working through this book. You're in control of your physical, mental, and emotional state. You know when and where to show up and what to bring with you. In other words, you're better prepared than most of the other people taking the GED® test with you. You're psyched.

Just one more thing. When you're finished with the test, you will have earned a reward. Plan a celebration. Call your friends and plan a party, have a nice dinner with your family, or pick out a movie to see—whatever your heart desires. Give yourself something to look forward to.

And then do it. Go into the test full of confidence, armed with test-taking strategies you've practiced until they're second nature. You're in control of yourself, your environment, and your performance on the exam. You're ready to succeed. So do it. Go in there and ace the test. And look forward to your future as someone who has successfully passed the GED® test!

Final Preparations

Getting to the Exam Site

Location of exam site: _____

Date of exam: _____

Departure time: _____

Do I know how to get to the exam site?   Yes ___   No ___

If No, make a trial run.

Time it will take to get to the exam site: _____

Things to Lay Out the Night Before

Clothes I will wear   _____

Sweater/jacket   _____

Watch   _____

Photo ID   _____

Four No. 2 pencils and
blue or black ink pens
(if taking the paper-
based test)   _____

Other Things to Bring/Remember

_____

_____

_____

_____

_____

_____

_____

_____

2 ▶ DIAGNOSTIC TEST

CHAPTER SUMMARY
This is the first of the three practice tests in this book based on the GED® Language Arts, Reading test. Use this test to see how you would do if you were to take the exam today.

This diagnostic practice exam is of the same type as the real GED® Language Arts, Reading test. Like the real test, it consists of 40 multiple-choice questions about reading passages. These questions test your skills in comprehension (extracting meaning), application (using information), analysis (breaking down information), and synthesis (putting elements together).

The answer sheet you should use for the multiple-choice questions is on the following page. Then comes the exam itself, and after that, the answer key. Each answer on the test is explained in the answer key to help you find out why the correct answers are right and why the incorrect answers are wrong.

Diagnostic Test

1.	ⓐ ⓑ ⓒ ⓓ ⓔ	18.	ⓐ ⓑ ⓒ ⓓ ⓔ	35.	ⓐ ⓑ ⓒ ⓓ ⓔ
2.	ⓐ ⓑ ⓒ ⓓ ⓔ	19.	ⓐ ⓑ ⓒ ⓓ ⓔ	36.	ⓐ ⓑ ⓒ ⓓ ⓔ
3.	ⓐ ⓑ ⓒ ⓓ ⓔ	20.	ⓐ ⓑ ⓒ ⓓ ⓔ	37.	ⓐ ⓑ ⓒ ⓓ ⓔ
4.	ⓐ ⓑ ⓒ ⓓ ⓔ	21.	ⓐ ⓑ ⓒ ⓓ ⓔ	38.	ⓐ ⓑ ⓒ ⓓ ⓔ
5.	ⓐ ⓑ ⓒ ⓓ ⓔ	22.	ⓐ ⓑ ⓒ ⓓ ⓔ	39.	ⓐ ⓑ ⓒ ⓓ ⓔ
6.	ⓐ ⓑ ⓒ ⓓ ⓔ	23.	ⓐ ⓑ ⓒ ⓓ ⓔ	40.	ⓐ ⓑ ⓒ ⓓ ⓔ
7.	ⓐ ⓑ ⓒ ⓓ ⓔ	24.	ⓐ ⓑ ⓒ ⓓ ⓔ	41.	ⓐ ⓑ ⓒ ⓓ ⓔ
8.	ⓐ ⓑ ⓒ ⓓ ⓔ	25.	ⓐ ⓑ ⓒ ⓓ ⓔ	42.	ⓐ ⓑ ⓒ ⓓ ⓔ
9.	ⓐ ⓑ ⓒ ⓓ ⓔ	26.	ⓐ ⓑ ⓒ ⓓ ⓔ	43.	ⓐ ⓑ ⓒ ⓓ ⓔ
10.	ⓐ ⓑ ⓒ ⓓ ⓔ	27.	ⓐ ⓑ ⓒ ⓓ ⓔ	44.	ⓐ ⓑ ⓒ ⓓ ⓔ
11.	ⓐ ⓑ ⓒ ⓓ ⓔ	28.	ⓐ ⓑ ⓒ ⓓ ⓔ	45.	ⓐ ⓑ ⓒ ⓓ ⓔ
12.	ⓐ ⓑ ⓒ ⓓ ⓔ	29.	ⓐ ⓑ ⓒ ⓓ ⓔ	46.	ⓐ ⓑ ⓒ ⓓ ⓔ
13.	ⓐ ⓑ ⓒ ⓓ ⓔ	30.	ⓐ ⓑ ⓒ ⓓ ⓔ	47.	ⓐ ⓑ ⓒ ⓓ ⓔ
14.	ⓐ ⓑ ⓒ ⓓ ⓔ	31.	ⓐ ⓑ ⓒ ⓓ ⓔ	48.	ⓐ ⓑ ⓒ ⓓ ⓔ
15.	ⓐ ⓑ ⓒ ⓓ ⓔ	32.	ⓐ ⓑ ⓒ ⓓ ⓔ	49.	ⓐ ⓑ ⓒ ⓓ ⓔ
16.	ⓐ ⓑ ⓒ ⓓ ⓔ	33.	ⓐ ⓑ ⓒ ⓓ ⓔ	50.	ⓐ ⓑ ⓒ ⓓ ⓔ
17.	ⓐ ⓑ ⓒ ⓓ ⓔ	34.	ⓐ ⓑ ⓒ ⓓ ⓔ		

Directions: Choose the *one best answer* to each question.

Questions 1 through 7 refer to the following excerpt from a novel.

Will Anne Miss Green Gables?

It was a happy and beautiful bride who came down the old carpeted stairs that September noon. She was the first bride of Green Gables, slender and shining-eyed, with her
(5) arms full of roses. Gilbert, waiting for her in the hall below, looked up at her with adoring eyes. She was his at last, this long-sought Anne, whom he won after years of patient waiting. It was to him she was coming. Was
(10) he worthy of her? Could he make her as happy as he hoped? If he failed her—if he could not measure up to her standards. . . .

But then, their eyes met and all doubt was swept away in a certainty that everything
(15) would be wonderful. They belonged to each other; no matter what life might hold for them, it could never alter that. Their happiness was in each other's keeping and both were unafraid.
(20) They were married in the sunshine of the old orchard, circled by the loving and kindly faces of long-familiar friends. Mr. Allan married them and the Reverend Jo made what Mrs. Rachel Lynde afterwards
(25) pronounced to be the "most beautiful wedding prayer" she had ever heard. Birds do not often sing in September, but one sang sweetly from some hidden tree while Gilbert and Anne repeated their vows. Anne heard it
(30) and thrilled to it. Gilbert heard it and wondered only that all the birds in the world had not burst into jubilant song. The bird sang until the ceremony was ended. Then it wound up with one more little, glad trill.
(35) Never had the old gray-green house among its enfolding orchards known a merrier afternoon. Laughter and joy had their way; and when Anne and Gilbert left to catch their train, Marilla stood at the gate
(40) and watched them drive out of sight down the long lane with its banks of goldenrod. Anne turned at its end to wave her last goodbye. She looked once more at her home and felt a tinge of sadness. Then she was
(45) gone—Green Gables was her home no more. It would never be again. Marilla's face looked very gray and old as she turned to the house which Anne had filled for years with light and life.

Adapted from L.M. Montgomery,
Anne's House of Dreams

1. Which of the following words best describes what Gilbert feels toward Anne?
   a. love
   b. fear
   c. respect
   d. gratitude
   e. nervousness

2. What happened when Gilbert's and Anne's eyes met?
   a. He wondered whether he was worthy of her.
   b. He thought his patience was worthwhile.
   c. He wondered what their life would be like.
   d. He realized they were meant for each other.
   e. He thought Anne would miss Green Gables very much.

3. Based on the excerpt, what was probably the hardest change for Anne?
   a. becoming a wife
   b. moving to another town
   c. saying goodbye to Marilla
   d. not being free to do what she wanted
   e. Green Gables not being her home any longer

4. Based on the excerpt, which description best characterizes the relationship between Marilla and Anne?

   a. Marilla felt tired from having taken care of Anne.

   b. Marilla raised Anne from childhood and cared about her.

   c. Marilla was sad that Anne left because she would have to leave, too.

   d. Marilla and Anne disagreed about Gilbert being a good husband.

   e. Marilla thought Anne was somewhat selfish by leaving her behind.

5. Which of the following best describes what the author means when she says "this long-sought Anne" (lines 7 and 8)?

   a. that Anne was no longer a young woman

   b. that Anne did not fall in love with Gilbert right away

   c. that Anne was patient with Gilbert

   d. that Anne had nearly married someone else

   e. that Anne had given Gilbert a difficult time

6. Of the characters in this excerpt, whose inner thoughts are hidden from the reader?

   a. Anne

   b. Gilbert

   c. Marilla

   d. Mr. Allan

   e. Mrs. Rachel Lynde

7. How does the bird's singing relate to Gilbert's and Anne's marriage?

   a. The bird's singing was distracting to those watching the service.

   b. The bird's singing mirrored the joy of the wedding service.

   c. The bird's singing seemed to suggest sad events in the future.

   d. The bird's singing was worrisome to the bridal couple.

   e. The bird's singing made it difficult to hear the vows.

Questions 8 through 13 refer to the following excerpt from a play.

Will They Weather the Storm of Life?

JENNY: [sitting at a table peeling potatoes when her husband, Danny, comes through the door of the one-room apartment; she takes one look at her husband and starts to

(5)   cry] Don't say it. You don't have to say it. I can see it on your face. You didn't get the job, did you?

DANNY: [putting his hand on Jenny's hand] I'm sorry. I waited in line for four hours in

(10)   that sun that beat down on all of us like an angry man. And then they told us all to go home. They said they had enough workers for now. They shut the gate and said to come back next week.

(15)   JENNY: Oh, what can we do? The landlord wants his rent. He came by today. I didn't know what to say to him. He's been kind to us, but his patience seems to be running out.

DANNY: I will talk to him. Maybe he will

(20)   give us more time.

JENNY: But he may not. What if he boots us out? What do we do then?

DANNY: We will do what so many others are doing: we will find a way. We have to.

(25)   President Roosevelt has some new programs

that may help us. I need to find out more about them. The government has to do something for us. This depression isn't our fault.

(30) JENNY: Maybe I could get another cleaning job. I will go to Mrs. Hayes tomorrow morning. She might know of another household that needs a good cleaner. Yes, that is what I will do.

(35) DANNY: But you work so hard already, with the washing you take in, and the sewing. If only I could find a job, I swear I would work harder than I've ever worked before.

JENNY: I will ask Mrs. Hayes about you, too.

(40) Perhaps they need another handy man to do odd jobs for them. I will ask her. She is kind. I will ask her. [Danny hugs his wife]

JENNY: Do you remember when we first got married? How many hopes we had for our

(45) lives. And now, it seems none of that will come true.

DANNY: Honey, we are young. Things will turn around. We need to keep going. We can't give up on our lives. You will see. We

(50) will have a better life one day. [he takes Jenny's hand in his]

8. Which of the following phrases best describes Jennifer?
  a. selfish and demanding
  b. quiet and passive
  c. determined and hopeful
  d. distressed and fearful
  e. comforting and cheering

9. Based on the information in this excerpt, how would Danny most likely behave if he had gotten the job?
  a. make sure that everyone in town knew
  b. accomplish a lot in a little time
  c. complain about how little the job pays
  d. quit after a few days of work
  e. ask for a raise after a few weeks

10. Which of the following best describes the mood of the scene?
  a. joyful
  b. excited
  c. terrified
  d. pleasant
  e. anxious

11. Which of the following is the most likely reason that Jennifer started to cry?
  a. She was worried about her husband being gone so long.
  b. She had an argument with the landlord about the rent.
  c. She was angry that her husband wasn't home.
  d. She was upset her husband didn't get the job.
  e. She felt sad about the long hours of work she had to do.

12. Based on the excerpt, what can be inferred about Jennifer's relationship to Mrs. Hayes?
  a. Jennifer is grateful to Mrs. Hayes.
  b. Jennifer dislikes Mrs. Hayes.
  c. Jennifer is envious of Mrs. Hayes.
  d. Jennifer is frightened of Mrs. Hayes.
  e. Jennifer is worried about Mrs. Hayes.

13. Based on the excerpt, which of the following is Danny most likely to do next?
  a. decide to leave his wife
  b. move to a new apartment
  c. check out the government programs
  d. have an argument with his landlord
  e. refuse to work for Mrs. Hayes

Questions 14 through 17 refer to the following excerpt from a short story.

Will He Appear on National Television?

"I think half the world has shown up for this audition." Gene was talking on his cell phone to his girlfriend. "I can't wait to perform. I know I'm in fine voice, and they are going to
(5)   love the song I chose."

"Well, good luck. I will be thinking of you."

Although he sounded upbeat with his girlfriend, in truth Gene was anything but
(10)   confident. He had staked so much on the audition, and he had no idea what the judges would really think of him. He realized for the first time that he was scared. Even so, he wanted to succeed so much he could almost
(15)   taste it. Just imagine competing on national television. He took a long breath in. It was hard to believe he was actually going to perform for the judges.

He had arrived exactly at nine and had
(20)   been in line for over three hours. He could hear his heart beating loudly. Right then, Gene heard his name being called. He went into the building and was ushered into the audition room.

(25)   "Yes, I'm here," he answered.

Gene looked at the judges sitting at the table. They seemed bored and unimpressed.

"Well, what are you going to sing for us today?" one of the judges asked him. "Time
(30)   after Time," Gene told him, his voice quavering a bit.

"Okay, let's see what you've got," said another judge who was tapping the table with a pencil.

(35)   Gene felt a knot in his throat and didn't know if he could go on. He remembered what his voice coach told him: "Just take a moment before you start. Close your eyes. Take a deep breath, and then let go." Gene
(40)   closed his eyes and took a breath and then a sweet voice began emanating from his mouth. The judges seemed to disappear. He could have been anywhere. He was in his own world.

(45)   Suddenly it was over, and he stood in front of the judges feeling very alone and vulnerable. He could feel the sweat on his brow.

"Well, that was a surprise," said the first
(50)   judge. "I never would have predicted that."

"What do you think? Does he go through?" All four of the judges gave him a thumbs up. "You're in, kid," the first judge said. "Don't make us regret our decision."

(55)   "Oh, no, sir. You won't regret it," Gene said as he nearly skipped out of the room.

14. Based on the excerpt, what does Gene most likely think about the audition?
   a. It will give him a chance to make a good living.
   b. It is something he had wanted to avoid.
   c. It is a chance for him to be discovered.
   d. It will be a good learning experience.
   e. It will make him famous in a short time.

15. When does the scene in this excerpt take place?
   a. early morning
   b. late afternoon
   c. early afternoon
   d. early evening
   e. late evening

16. Which is the best description of Gene's performance?
   a. a good try but not good enough
   b. a fine voice but without true conviction
   c. a bit slow to start but ultimately wonderful
   d. a showy voice but not much rhythm
   e. a scratchy voice but one that showed promise

17. What is the main effect of the author's use of phrases such as "could almost taste it," "took a long breath in," and "beating loudly"?
   a. to show how long Gene had been waiting
   b. to show that Gene was tired
   c. to show that Gene was talented
   d. to show that Gene had been exercising
   e. to show how important the audition was to Gene

Questions 18 through 23 refer to the following excerpt from a poem.

What Was Her Life About?

(1)   We were married and lived together for
             seventy years,
(2)   Enjoying, working, raising twelve children,
(3)   Eight of whom we lost
(4)   Ere I had reached the age of sixty.
(5)   I spun, wove, kept the house, nursed the sick,
(6)   Made the garden, and for the holiday
(7)   Rambled over the fields where sang many larks,
(8)   And by the Spoon River gathering many a shell,
(9)   And many a flower and medicinal weed—
(10) Shouting to the wooded hills, singing to the
             green valleys.
(11) At ninety-six I had lived enough, that is all,
(12) And passed a sweet repose.
             Edgar Lee Masters, *Spoon River Anthology*

18. Based on the excerpt, what does the woman mean when she talks of "passing a sweet repose" (line 12)?
   a. her death
   b. her old age
   c. how well she slept at night
   d. needing to rest more as she grew older
   e. her dreams

19. Which of the following words best describes the overall mood of the poem?
   a. joy
   b. anger
   c. acceptance
   d. wonder
   e. dreaminess

20. Which of the following is the most likely explanation of the line from the poem that reads, "Shouting to the wooded hills, singing to the green valleys" (line 10)?
   a. The speaker had a fine singing voice.
   b. The speaker loved the countryside.
   c. The speaker preferred sounds to silence.
   d. The speaker spent of a lot of time working in the fields.
   e. The speaker tried to become famous.

21. Which can you infer about the couple's marriage?
   a. They were never meant to be together.
   b. They could not deal with the loss of their children.
   c. They had an extremely happy marriage.
   d. They had their sorrows and their joys.
   e. They were very different in old age.

22. If the woman could give advice to a young bride, which of the following would the woman most likely say?
   a. Always try to be happy, no matter what.
   b. Life is filled with pain.
   c. Have your own interests.
   d. Marriage is wonderful.
   e. Take life in stride.

23. Which of the following best describes the woman's conclusions about her own death?

   a. She regretted not having done more with her life.

   b. She wanted to live a bit longer to see her grandchildren grown.

   c. She had lived a full life, and it was time for her to die.

   d. She felt resentful that she had so little time with her husband.

   e. She wished she had died when her husband did.

Questions 24 through 29 refer to the following employee memo.

What Will the New Procedures Do?

Memo

To: Employees of IMPEL

From: Management

Re: New Security Procedures

(5)   Date: June 15

As a result of some incidents that have occurred with unauthorized persons in secure parts of Building A, as of June 30, new procedures will go into effect for security in

(10)   that building. From now on, all employees reporting to work should enter through the employee entrance at the side of the building on Murray Street. No employee is to enter through the main entrance. In order to be

(15)   admitted, each employee must have a valid photo ID. The ID needs to be swiped to unlock the door. Make sure not to allow another person to enter with you even if you know the person. Each employee needs to

(20)   swipe his or her own ID in order to be registered as being on the job.

The main entrance will be for visitors only. The receptionist there will call the party that the visitor is coming to meet so that he

(25)   or she can come to the main desk to escort the guest to his or her office. Visitors will be given temporary passes, but they cannot have full run of the office.

In addition, all employees will also be

(30)   required to log in on their computer when they begin work and log out when they take a break. Make sure to log out and in when taking lunch breaks.

If an employee sees someone whom he

(35)   or she believes is unauthorized to be in Building A, that employee should take immediate action and report the event to Mr. Shields, our head of security. Do not approach the person, but simply call Mr.

(40)   Shields's office. His extension is 890. If there is no answer, make a written report and e-mail it to cshields@impel.com.

If employees have any questions regarding these regulations, please contact

(45)   the Human Resources department at extension 550. Ms. Hardy will be able to respond to your queries. Thank you for your cooperation in this matter. We feel that with these additional procedures, our workplace

(50)   will be made more secure for everyone concerned. Ideally, this will result in improved work output, since any possibility of a security breach will be prevented.

24. Which of the following best restates the phrase "security breach" (line 53)?

   a. a compromise in the safety of the office

   b. a blow to the confidence of employees

   c. a distraction because of an employee's personal problems

   d. a defense against employees not doing their jobs

   e. a guarantee that the office is safe

25. Based on the excerpt, which of the following can be inferred about management?
   a. They are concerned about the safety of employees.
   b. They believe that the office is completely secure.
   c. They want employees to fill out time sheets.
   d. They want to track employee work habits.
   e. They are considering giving some employees raises.

26. Which of the following could be prevented by the new security procedures?
   a. visitors entering through the main entrance
   b. employees swiping IDs to open doors
   c. employees entering through the side entrance
   d. unauthorized persons wandering around Building A
   e. employees not working hard enough

27. Imagine an employee sees a person in Building A without an ID badge. According to the memo, which of these actions should the employee take?
   a. go to Mr. Shields's office at once
   b. call Mr. Shields's office to make a report
   c. tell the person to leave the building
   d. call the receptionist in the main entrance
   e. report the event to Ms. Hardy

28. Which of the following best describes the style in which this memo is written?
   a. complicated and unclear
   b. academic and dry
   c. amusing and humorous
   d. straightforward and direct
   e. detailed and technical

29. Which of the following best describes the way in which the memo is organized?
   a. by listing information in the order of importance
   b. by sequence of events
   c. by presenting a problem and then a solution
   d. by comparing and contrasting issues
   e. by stating the most relevant points first and the least relevant last

Questions 30 through 35 refer to the following excerpt from a novel.

Will His Mother Let Him Leave?

"Beatrice," he said suddenly, "I want to go away to school. Everybody in Minneapolis is going to go away to school."

Beatrice showed some alarm.

(5)   "But you're only fifteen."

"Yes, but everybody goes away to school at fifteen, and I *want* to, Beatrice."

On Beatrice's suggestion, the subject was dropped for the rest of the walk, but a
(10) week later she delighted him by saying, "Amory, I have decided to let you have your way. If you still want to, you can go away to school."

"Yes?"

(15)   "To St. Regis's in Connecticut."

Amory said nothing, but he felt a bolt of excitement along his spine.

"It's being arranged," continued Beatrice. "It's better that you should go away.
(20) I'd have preferred you to have gone to Eton and then to Christ Church, Oxford. But it seems impracticable now—and for the present, we'll let the university question take care of itself."

(25)   "What are you going to do, Beatrice?"

"Heaven knows. It seems my fate to spend my years in this country. Not for a second do I regret being American—indeed,

(30) I think that regret is very typical of ignorant people. I feel sure we are the great coming nation, yet"—and she sighed, "I feel my life should have slipped away close to an older, mellower civilization, a land of greens and autumnal browns. . . ."

(35) Amory did not answer, so his mother continued, "My regret is that you haven't been abroad. But still, as you are a man, it's better that you should grow up here under the snarling eagle—is that the right term?"

(40) Amory agreed that it was.

"When do I go to school?"

"Next month. You'll have to start East a little early to take your examinations. After that you'll have a free week, so I want you to

(45) go up the Hudson and pay a visit."

"To who?"

"To Monsignor Darcy, Amory. He wants to see you. He went to Harrow and then to Yale—became a Catholic. I want him

(50) to talk to you. I feel he can be such a help." She stroked his auburn hair gently. "Dear Amory, dear Amory. . . ."

Adapted from F. Scott Fitzgerald,
This Side of Paradise

30. Which of the following best expresses the main idea of the excerpt?
   a. a boy's mother agrees to let her son go to a boarding school
   b. a boy's mother would like her son to visit schools in other countries
   c. a boy wants to make his mother happy
   d. a boy wants to get away from his hometown
   e. a boy's mother wants her son to go to school at home

31. Based on the information in this excerpt, which of the following would Beatrice most likely prefer to do?
   a. learn about American history
   b. have a potluck dinner with friends
   c. spend time in England
   d. teach English to schoolchildren
   e. travel throughout the United States

32. Why does Beatrice most likely think it is better for Amory to grow up in America?
   a. He would not like Europe.
   b. He is good at sports.
   c. It is where his father lives.
   d. Schools are easier in America.
   e. He was born in America.

33. Based on Beatrice saying "I feel my life should have slipped away close to an older, mellower civilization, a land of greens and autumnal browns" (lines 31 to 34), what does she suggest about America?
   a. She thinks it is similar to England.
   b. She believes it is a land of great energy.
   c. She assumes it is a weak country with little future.
   d. She decides then to adopt it as her home.
   e. She wants to make England a stronger nation.

34. How does Amory calling his mother by her first name influence the excerpt?
   a. It shows that Amory and his mother are not close.
   b. It shows that Beatrice wants to appear to be Amory's sister.
   c. It shows that Beatrice resents being a mother.
   d. It shows that Amory is disrespectful of his mother.
   e. It shows that Amory and his mother's relationship is not typical.

35. Why does Beatrice want Amory to visit Monsignor Darcy?
  a. Amory dreams of attending college at Yale.
  b. She thinks that Monsignor Darcy can convince Amory to go to school closer to home.
  c. Monsignor Darcy is Amory's uncle.
  d. She wants Amory to become Catholic.
  e. She feels that Monsignor Darcy can help Amory because he went to Harrow and Yale.

Questions 36 through 40 refer to the following excerpt from a review.

What Does the Reviewer Think of *Last Fight*?

Last Fight may be one of the biggest blockbusters of the summer, but it doesn't live up to the buzz around it. In this science fiction tale of epic proportions, viewers are
(5)   propelled forward to a future when Earth is populated by androids and humans. These survivors of an ancient civilization live in a sterile world covered by a plastic dome. The dome is for protection from aliens who
(10)   attack Earth on a regular basis. It also cuts down on such environmental problems as air pollution and global warming.

        The plot centers around a young man named Raal and his quest to forge a peace
(15)   between the humans and the aliens. His is a difficult task, considering the aliens have no desire to stop trying to overcome Earth and its inhabitants. While Raal (George Armstrong) is a likeable character, he lacks the ability to
(20)   change expression to any extent. As a result, his acting range is quite limited. He is something of a dreamer, and perhaps the message here is that there is no place for dreamers in the future, but I will not detail
(25)   the plot or the ending. I don't want to spoil it

for those people who may actually want to view the film. Still, let it be said that events do not go well for young Raal.

        The high point of the movie for me
(30)   was the performance by veteran actor Bruce Cameron as the sage Kel. He has shown over and over his ability to transform even the most mundane character into someone fascinating to watch. It may be worth seeing
(35)   the film just for his performance.

        Besides being far-fetched, the movie concentrates too much on special effects, including 3-D, but that of course may be a draw for many viewers. Its cost was also
(40)   enormous. Not much that is green is in this film.

36. Which of the following is the main idea of the excerpt?
  a. The author is giving the reasons movies should not use special effects.
  b. The author is detailing the kind of acting that he prefers.
  c. The author is providing his impressions of a science fiction movie.
  d. The author is explaining why he enjoys science fiction movies.
  e. The author is warning people about the violence in the movie.

37. Which of the following best expresses the reviewer's opinion of *Last Fight*?
  a. It was too expensive to make and is too long.
  b. It was enjoyable because there was some great acting in it.
  c. The reviewer hopes that most people will turn out for the movie.
  d. It has little depth and relies too much on special effects.
  e. A sequel to the movie might have better acting.

38. If it is known that the author of this review had written numerous science fiction scripts, none of which were ever made into a movie, how would this most likely affect the reading of this review?
  a. The experiences of the author give his or her opinion greater value.
  b. The author's knowledge of the genre may be questioned.
  c. Much of the negativity might be construed as sour grapes.
  d. Some of the criticism could be explained as idle gossip.
  e. The author's personal experiences have no influence on the review whatsoever.

39. Which of the following best describes the style in which this review is written?
  a. technical
  b. humorous
  c. straightforward
  d. simple
  e. ornate

40. According to the author, which word best describes *Last Fight*?
  a. provocative
  b. lighthearted
  c. solemn
  d. overblown
  e. uneven

Answers

Will Anne Miss Green Gables?

1. a. Although Gilbert may feel *respect* and *gratitude*, the word that best describes his feelings is **love**. It is clearly indicated in his actions. *Nervousness* is not supported by the excerpt, nor is *fear*.

2. d. This choice is clearly supported by what the excerpt says happened when their eyes met— "and all doubt was swept away in a certainty that everything would be wonderful." The other choices may enter into the scene between them, but they do not occur when their eyes met.

3. e. It is clear from the ending of the excerpt that this was the biggest and hardest change for Anne. That is why she felt a "tinge of sadness." The other choices are not supported.

4. b. There are hints in the excerpt that support this answer, such as Marilla looking "gray" when Anne was leaving and how Anne had filled the house with "light and life." The other choices are not supported by the text.

5. b. Based on the information in the excerpt, this is the correct answer. The text says that Gilbert had won her "after years of patient waiting." This supports choice b, not the other choices.

6. d. The author gives the readers clues about what all the other characters are thinking, but the reader does not learn anything about Mr. Allan.

7. b. The text says that not many birds sang in September but that one sang sweetly while Gilbert and Anne repeated their vows. It even "wound up with one more little, glad trill" after the ceremony was over, seeming to mirror the joy of the wedding service.

Will They Weather the Storm of Life?

8. d. This is the best answer. Jenny seems **distressed and fearful** about their situation and worries about the future. She is not *hopeful* nor is she *cheering*. She is not *passive* since she is trying to find a job for her husband, and she shows that she is not *selfish* by offering to get another job.

9. b. Danny wants to get a job; he waited in line for four hours. He says he would work harder than ever before if he gets a job. This is the only choice that is supported by the text.

10. e. Danny and Jenny cannot pay their rent. Danny cannot get a job, and Jenny is worried about the future. This choice is supported by the text. The mood is not *joyful*, nor is it *pleasant*. However, while the mood is not *excited*, it is hardly *terrified*.

11. d. Based on the excerpt, Jennifer started to cry because her husband did not get a job, not because she has to work long hours. While she is probably upset about the landlord, that was not the direct reason for her crying.

12. a. From what Jenny says about Mrs. Hayes, the reader can tell that she is grateful to her. Jenny is even thinking of asking Mrs. Hayes whether she has work for her husband. She also says that Mrs. Hayes is kind. She does not seem to dislike her. Jenny does not seem envious either, and she certainly does not seem to be afraid of or worried about her.

13. c. Based on the excerpt, logically he is most likely to do this. He talks about the new government programs and that he wants to find out more about them. He probably would not want to have a fight with his landlord, nor would he want to leave his wife, whom he seems to love. The other choices are not likely, either.

Will He Appear on National Television?

14. c. This is the best answer. The audition will give him a chance to be discovered. The audition will not make him become famous. It might be a good learning situation, but that is not the primary reason that Gene is there.

15. c. The excerpt says Gene got to the audition site at 9:00 a.m. and had been waiting more than three hours (line 20). That would make the time after noon.

16. c. This answer reflects what happens in the story. At first he was slow to start, but then he sang very well and passed the round of auditions.

17. e. This answer reflects the feelings that Gene was having about the audition. For instance, a person's heart often beats loudly—or seems to beat louder than usual—when a person is experiencing an important moment in life.

What Was Her Life About?

18. a. Based on the excerpt, the reader can determine that the woman is talking about her death. The other choices do not fit in with the context of the poem.

19. c. This is the best answer. The speaker tells about her life in a matter-of-fact manner. She does not seem to be in a state of *wonder* or *dreaminess*. She certainly does not seem *angry* or particularly full of *joy*.

20. b. The line suggests that the speaker loved nature. It does not suggest that she worked in the fields or that she had a fine singing voice. No other choice is supported by the poem.

21. d. The poem recounts what occurred in their marriage, both good and bad, so this is the best answer. The other choices are not supported by the poem.

22. e. This seems to be the most logical answer. The speaker is very candid about her life and seems to have taken things in stride herself. The other choices are not overall themes supported by the lines of the poem.

23. c. The woman says that she "had lived enough, and that is all," which suggests that she lived a full life and that it was time for her to die. There's no mention of regret or living to see her grandchildren, and there is nothing about her wanting to die when her husband did.

What Will the New Procedures Do?

24. a. This phrase means that the security was somehow broken, so choice **a** is correct. This can be seen in the very first section of the memo: "As a result of some incidents that have occurred with unauthorized persons in secure parts. . . ." The other choices are not suggested by these words. They have nothing to do with security being compromised.

25. a. The point of the memo is that there were some security incidents that needed to be addressed. Based on the memo, choice **b** is clearly not correct, and the others are not suggested by the memo, either.

26. d. If you read the memo carefully, you will see that this is the one option that the new regulations will help prevent. It is mentioned in the first paragraph.

27. b. Again, a close reading of the text will reveal that this is what an employee is to do first if a stranger is seen in Building A. This can be found in the third paragraph.

28. d. The memo is direct and to the point. It is not technical, and it certainly isn't humorous. It's quite clear and not at all academic.

29. c. The memo states a problem at the beginning and then describes the new regulations that will solve it—a way to keep unauthorized persons out of secure parts of Building A.

Will His Mother Let Him Leave?

30. a. This choice is clearly correct. It contains the main idea of the excerpt. The dialogue is about a boy wanting to go away to school and his mother finally agreeing to it.

31. c. It seems clear from the dialogue in the excerpt that Beatrice would prefer to be in England rather than do any of the other activities. She seems not to mind America, but she does long for her native country.

32. e. This is the most logical choice, although it is never actually stated in the excerpt. There is no mention of the father, although he may or may not live in America. The other choices are not supported by the passage, either.

33. b. This is the only choice suggested by the lines spoken by Beatrice. She is comparing England's mellow nature to America's energetic spirit.

34. e. This is the best and most all-encompassing answer. This mother and son do not seem like most mothers and sons. The way they relate and talk suggests an atypical relationship.

35. e. This is the most obvious reason that Beatrice wants Amory to meet Monsignor Darcy. She says he went to Harrow and Yale, and she wants Amory to talk to him.

What Does the Reviewer Think of *Last Fight*?

36. c. This is what the review is mostly about. The reviewer does address the other answer choices, but they do not represent the main intent of the review.

37. d. Based on what the reviewer says about the movie, this is the best answer. The reviewer does not mention a sequel, although he does say the acting is bad. He does not mention the length of the film, either.

38. c. This is the most logical choice. People reading the review would take into consideration that the reviewer has never had any of his or her science fiction scripts made into a movie. This would definitely taint the review, as he or she might be overly critical.

39. b. The review is somewhat *humorous*, or at least that is its intention. Although the 3-D aspect of the film is mentioned, that's not really enough to call the review *technical*. A technical review would probably have discussed the 3-D aspect at more length. None of the other choices properly describe the writing style of the review.

40. d. This word best describes what the reviewer feels about the movie. Overall, the reviewer is not very impressed with the film, so a positive choice like **b** could be eliminated. None of the other choices accurately describes the author's opinion.

Diagnostic Bloom Thinking Skill Analysis

The question numbers below correspond to the skill being tested.

	Comprehension	Application	Analysis	Synthesis
Nonfiction	24, 36, 40	26, 27	25, 37	28, 29, 38, 39
Fiction	1, 2, 14, 15, 30	3, 31	4, 5, 6, 32, 33	7, 16, 17,34,35
Poetry	18	22	20, 21	19, 23
Drama	8	9	11, 12, 13	10

CHAPTER

3 ▶ ESSENTIAL READING SKILLS

CHAPTER SUMMARY
This chapter will help you build the foundation you need to understand the fiction and nonfiction passages found on the GED® Language Arts, Reading test. You will learn to identify word parts, prefixes, suffixes, context clues, multiple word meanings, the author's point of view and purpose, and theme. It will also teach you to make predictions and synthesize what you read.

The key to doing well on the GED® Language Arts, Reading test is being able to comprehend what you read. Some questions will require you to simply recall facts and information that you have read. However, a number of questions require a much deeper understanding of the text.

Fiction passages make up three-fourths of the GED® Language Arts, Reading test; these passages will either be prose, poetry, or drama. Nonfiction passages make up the remaining one-fourth. In this chapter, you will review comprehension skills needed to understand these passages. Keep in mind that the skills reviewed in this chapter are also important in comprehending literature in general.

Word Parts

To understand what a passage is about, you have to be able to determine the meanings of its words. Words are formed from a combination of root words, prefixes, and suffixes. **Root words** are the foundation of words.

Prefixes are added to the beginning of words to change their meanings. **Suffixes** are added to the ends of words to change their meanings.

Look at the following example:

unexpected = un + expect + ed

In the word *unexpected, un-* is the prefix, *expect* is the root word, and *-ed* is the suffix. Each of these parts works together to give the word meaning. Think about the differences in the meanings of the following sentences:

> *We expect her to call by 1:00 today.*
> *We expected her to call by noon yesterday.*
> *The fact that she did not call was unexpected.*

Adding the suffix *-ed* to the end of the word changes it to past tense. Adding the prefix *un-* to the beginning tells that the event was *not* expected.

> *Mario is an honest man.*

Let's look at the underlined word, *honest*. We know that honest means "truthful" or "trustworthy." So, the sentence lets us know that Mario can be trusted.

> *Mario is a dishonest man.*

In this sentence, the prefix *dis-* has been added to the root word *honest*. This prefix means "not," so we know that *dishonest* means "not honest." Adding the prefix has changed the meaning of the sentence. Now we know that Mario cannot be trusted.

> *Emily handled the package with care.*
> *Emily was careless with the package.*

The first sentence tells that Emily was gentle with the package. However, when the suffix *-less* is added to the root word *care*, the meaning changes. This suffix means "without," so *careless* means "without care."

> *Emily was careful with the package.*

This sentence uses the same root, *care*, but adds the suffix *-ful*. This suffix means "full of," so Emily was full of care when she handled the package.

Following are lists of some common prefixes and suffixes and their meanings. Knowing the meanings of these word parts can help you figure out meanings of words and help you better understand what you read.

Prefixes

- *co-*: with
- *de-*: to take away
- *dis-*: lack of, opposite of
- *ex-*: out of, previous
- *extra-*: outside, beyond
- *il-, in-, im-, ir-*: not
- *inter-*: between, among
- *mis-*: wrongly, badly
- *non-*: without, not
- *pre-*: before
- *post-*: after
- *re-*: again
- *sub-*: lower, nearly, under
- *super-*: above, over
- *trans-*: across
- *un-*: not

Suffixes

- *-able, -ible*: able to, can be done
- *-ant*: one who
- *-en*: made of
- *-er*: comparative, one who
- *-ful*: full of
- *-ive*: likely to
- *-ize*: to make
- *-less*: without
- *-ly*: in a certain way
- *-ment*: action, process
- *-ness, -ity*: state of
- *-or*: one who
- *-ous*: full of
- *-tion*: act, process

Now, use what you know about word parts to determine the meaning of the underlined word in the following sentence. Write the meaning of the word on the line underneath.

> *It seemed illogical for her to drop out of the campaign.*

_____

Breaking the underlined word into word parts can help determine its meaning. The word *illogical* is made up of the prefix *il-*, meaning "not," and the word *logical*. If something is logical, it makes sense. So, if it is illogical, it does not make sense.

Sometimes, thinking of a word with a similar root can help you figure out the meaning of an unfamiliar word.

The captain watched the sails deflate as he attempted to guide the boat to the dock.

Suppose you do not know the meaning of *deflate*. Ask yourself, "Do I know a word that has a similar root?" You probably already know that *inflate* means to fill something with air or to make something larger.

Dad will inflate the balloons before the party.

Using what you know about the meanings of word parts, you can figure out that *deflate* means that the air has gone out of something, or it has gotten smaller.

Let's try another example:

Brian carries his portable CD player everywhere he goes.

Portable contains the root *port* and the suffix *-able*. *Port* means "to move," so *portable* means that the CD player is "able to be moved."

The company plans to export 75% of its products overseas.

Suppose you are unsure of the meaning of *export*. Do you know a word that has a similar root? *Portable* and *export* have the same root. You know that the prefix in *export*, *ex-*, means "out of" and *port* means "to move," so *export* means "to move out." So, the company plans to move its products out and send them overseas.

The island imports most of its fruit from other countries.

If *export* means "to move out," what do you think *import* means? It means "to move in" or "to bring in."

Now you try. What words could help you determine the meaning of the underlined word in the following sentence? Write the words on the line underneath.

She tried to visualize the author's description of the animal.

_____

Vision and *visible* both have roots that are similar to that of *visualize*. *Vision* is the sense of sight. If something is *visible*, it is able to be seen. So, to *visualize* means "to see something."

Here are a few sets of words with similar roots. Knowing sets of words with similar roots can help you determine word meanings. What other words could you add to each set in the list below? What other groups of words can you think of that have similar roots?

- adjoin, conjunction, juncture
- anniversary, annual, biannual

- audible, audience, audio
- benevolent, benefit, beneficial
- chronic, chronological, synchronize
- civic, civilian, civilization
- contradict, dictate, dictionary
- describe, prescribe, transcribe
- design, signal, signature
- empathy, pathetic, sympathy
- evacuate, vacancy, vacuum
- exclaim, exclamation, proclaim
- mystify, mystery, mysterious
- pollutant, pollute, pollution
- telescope, telephone, television
- terrain, terrestrial, territory

Context Clues

Even great readers will come across unfamiliar words in a text at times. One way to figure out the meanings of these words is to use **context clues**. These are hints that are included in the sentence or passage that help readers understand the meanings of words.

Authors often use **synonyms**, or words with similar meanings, to help readers understand unfamiliar terms.

Beginning this semester, students will have an underlined abbreviated, or shortened, day every Wednesday.

In this sentence, the author included the synonym *shortened* to explain what he or she means by *abbreviated*. This context clue helps readers determine the meaning of a word that might be unfamiliar.

An author might also include **antonyms**, or words with opposite meanings, to clarify the definition of a word.

Please be advised that both residents and visitors are expected to park their cars on the west side of the apartment building.

This sentence talks about *residents* and *visitors*. So, we can conclude that residents are different than visitors. Because you probably know that visitors are people who do not live in the building, we can figure out that *residents* are people who do live there.

Definitions or **explanations** are often used as context clues.

The reluctant child was not eager to share his project with the class.

In this sentence, the author explained the meaning of *reluctant* by saying that the child was *not eager*.

Examples are another type of context clue that can be used to determine the meaning of unknown words.

Ms. Greene pointed out pictures of several monuments in the students' history books, including the Statue of Liberty, the Lincoln Memorial, and the Liberty Bell.

This sentence includes three examples of monuments: the Statue of Liberty, the Lincoln Memorial, and the Liberty Bell. From these examples, we can figure out that a *monument* must be a famous place or structure that has a special importance.

TIP

When looking for context clues, be sure to check sentences surrounding the unfamiliar word. These clues might be contained in the sentences before or after the sentence that includes the word in question, or they may even be in another part of the paragraph.

As you read the sentences below, look for context clues that could help you determine the meanings of the underlined words. Then, answer the questions that follow.

> *We climbed all day before reaching the apex, or top, of the mountain. We hadn't eaten anything in several hours and were all famished. I was so extremely hungry that I couldn't wait for lunch. As we ate our picnic, we talked about many topics, some frivolous, others serious. After an hour of eating, relaxing, and enjoying the gorgeous view, we began our hike back down the trail.*

1. What is the meaning of *apex*?

_____

2. What clues helped you determine the meaning?

_____

The synonym *top* probably helped you figure out that *apex* means the top, or the highest point, of the mountain.

3. What is the meaning of *famished*?

_____

4. What clues helped you determine the meaning?

_____

The sentence explains that the hikers hadn't eaten anything in several hours. The following sentence includes the definition "extremely hungry." These context clues probably helped you figure out that *famished* means "extremely hungry" or "starving." Notice that some of the clues were in the sentence following the underlined word. Also, notice that clues were found in more than one place. Be sure to look throughout the entire paragraph for clues that can help you determine meaning.

5. What is the meaning of *frivolous*?

_____

6. What clues helped you determine the meaning?

_____

The paragraph states that some of the topics the hikers discussed were *frivolous* and others were *serious*. This use of an antonym tells us that something that is *frivolous* is not serious.

Multiple Meaning Words

Many words have more than one meaning. As we read, it is important to know which meaning the author intends to use. Consider the use of the word *stoop* in the following sentences:

> *Li sat on the front stoop, waiting for her neighbor to come home.*

> *David had to stoop to fit into the tiny door of his little brother's clubhouse.*

> *The other candidate is constantly telling lies, but I would never stoop so low.*

In the first sentence, *stoop* means "a small porch." In the second sentence, *stoop* means "to bend forward." In the third sentence, *stoop* means "to do something unethical."

So, if words have more than one meaning, how are you supposed to figure out which is correct? You'll have to use context clues. Think about which definition makes sense in that particular sentence.

Read the following sentence.

> *The detective said the intruders left without a trace.*

Which is the meaning of *trace* in this sentence?

    a. a tiny amount
    b. a remaining sign
    c. a type of drawing
    d. to find something
    e. to copy something

In the sentence, the detective could not find any remaining sign that the intruders had been there. Although each of the answer choices is a definition of *trace*, only answer **b** makes sense in the context of the sentence.

Author's Purpose

To fully understand what we read, we need to be able to figure out why the passage was written. An author always has a reason, or purpose, for writing. The **author's purpose** for writing a passage is usually one of the following:

- to entertain
- to inform
- to persuade

Understanding the author's reason for writing can help you better understand what you read. Different types of texts usually have different purposes. Many stories, plays, magazine articles, poems, novels, and comic strips are written to **entertain**. They may be fiction or nonfiction and may include facts, opinions, or both, but the purpose for writing them is to tell a story. These are intended to entertain readers and are meant for pleasure reading.

This summer while vacationing in Florida, I went parasailing with my mom. It was the most thrilling adventure I'd ever had! We floated from a giant parachute, hundreds of feet above the water, and soared over the beaches.

This passage was written to entertain. It was intended to tell a story about the author's adventure. It does not try to teach any information, nor does it try to convince you to share an opinion about the topic.

Textbooks, encyclopedias, and many newspaper articles are written to **inform**. Their purpose is to give the reader information or to teach about a subject. Such passages will usually contain mostly facts and may include charts, diagrams, or drawings to help explain the information.

Parasailing is a sport in which a rider is attached to a large parachute, or parasail. The parasail is attached to a vehicle, usually a boat, by a long tow rope. As the boat moves, the parasail and rider rise up into the air.

This paragraph teaches readers about the sport of parasailing. It contains facts and information about the topic. Readers may enjoy reading about the subject, but the author's reason for writing the passage was to inform.

Other material, such as commercials, advertisements, letters to the editor, and political speeches, are written to **persuade** readers to share a belief, agree with an opinion, or support an idea. Such writing may include some facts or statements from experts, but it will most likely include the author's opinions about the topic.

One of the most dangerous sports today is parasailing. Each year, many people are seriously injured, or even killed, while participating in this activity. Laws should be passed that prohibit such reckless entertainment. If people want to fly, they should get on an airplane.

The author of this paragraph wants to convince readers that parasailing is a dangerous sport. The text not only includes opinions, but also facts that support the author's stand on the subject. Notice that strong words and phrases, such as *seriously injured*, *should*, and *reckless*, are included to stir up emotions in the readers. The author's purpose for writing this passage was to persuade readers to agree with his or her beliefs about parasailing.

BOOST

Did you know that the GED® test was originally created for military personnel and veterans who did not finish high school? That was in 1942. Five years later, New York became the first state to make the test available to civilians. By 1974, the GED® test was available in all 50 U.S. states.

Let's practice what you've learned about recognizing the author's purpose. Read the paragraph and determine whether it was written to entertain, inform, or persuade.

It was a quiet summer evening. The moon was full, and the sky seemed to hold a million stars. Outside, only the sounds of the crickets could be heard.

What was the author's purpose for writing this passage?

Did you recognize that the author's purpose was to entertain? The text did not try to teach anything or convince you to hold a certain opinion. It was simply written for the reader to enjoy.

Point of View

It is important to think about who is telling the story. This narrator may be someone who is a part of the story, or it may be someone outside of the events. The **point of view** refers to who is telling the story, which makes a difference in how much information the reader is given.

Some stories use a **first-person** point of view. In this case, one of the characters is telling the story, and readers see the events through this person's eyes.

After the game, Henry and I grabbed a pizza with the rest of the team. We hung out for a couple of hours, then headed home. By then, I was totally exhausted.

Notice that when an author uses a first-person point of view, the narrator uses the pronouns *I*, *me*, *us*, and *we*, and it seems as if the character is speaking directly to the reader. The narrator only knows his or her own thoughts and feelings, not those of the other characters, and often shares his or her attitudes and opinions with the readers.

Other stories use a **third-person** point of view, in which the narrator is not a character in the story and does not participate in the events.

After the game, Deon said he would join Henry and the rest of the team for pizza. They stayed for a couple of hours before heading home, exhausted.

When a story is told from the third-person point of view, the narrator will use pronouns such as *he*, *she*, and *they* when discussing the characters. Also, the narrator often knows the thoughts and feelings of every character.

Let's practice what you've just reviewed. Read the next three paragraphs, think about who is telling the story, and determine the point of view of the passage.

As soon as the bell rang, a tall, thin woman with dark hair rose from behind the desk. The class quieted as she began to speak.

"Good morning, class," she stated. "I am Ms. Wolfe, and I will be your English teacher this semester. Go ahead and open your books to the table of contents, and let's get started."

Ms. Wolfe picked up the text from her desk, and opened it to the first page.

What is the point of view of this passage?

_____

This passage is written in the third-person point of view. The narrator is not a character in the story. Notice that the pronoun *I* is included in the passage. However, it is spoken by one of the characters, not the narrator.

Theme

As we read, we look for and try to understand the messages and information that the author wants to share. Sometimes, the author's message is very obvious. Other times, we have to look a little harder to find it. The **theme** of a story is its underlying message. In a fable, the moral of the story is the theme. In fiction, this overall message is usually implied, rather than being directly stated, and may involve the following:

- attitudes
- beliefs
- opinions
- perceptions

The theme often leaves you with ideas, a conclusion, or a lesson that the writer wants you to take away from the story. Often, this lesson relates to life, society, or human nature. As you read, think about what the author's message might be. Consider the characters' words and actions, the tone, the plot, and any repeated patterns to see what views of the writer these portray.

Think about the story of the three little pigs. One could say that the theme of this story is that it is best to do a job the right way the first time. The author does not directly state this message, but this is a lesson or opinion that readers might take away from the story.

Common themes you may have found in reading might include:

- Crime does not pay.
- It is important to be honest.
- Be happy with what you have.
- Money cannot buy happiness.
- Keep going when things get tough.
- Do not be afraid to try something new.

Give it a try. Look for the theme as you read the passage below.

Camilla usually looked forward to Friday nights, but this week was the definite exception. Instead of going to the movies with her friends, she would be stuck at home, helping Mom get ready for tomorrow's garage sale. As she walked into the house, Camilla could see that Mom was already prepared for the long night ahead of them.

"Hey, get that scowl off your face and throw on your overalls," Mom called out cheerfully. "It won't be that bad."

Camilla changed clothes and headed to the garage, dragging her feet the whole way. Mom was elbow deep in an old cardboard box. She pulled out a raggedy, old stuffed dog.

"Mr. Floppy!" Camilla cried, excited to see her old friend. "I haven't seen him in years!"

"Your very first soft friend," Mom reminisced. "I'm assuming you'll be keeping him? Or would you like a 25-cent price tag to stick on his ear?"

Camilla set the old dog aside. She would definitely keep him. She helped Mom empty the rest of the box, sticking price tags on other old toys and books. They continued through the boxes, stopping to look through old photo albums together, telling funny stories about some of the useless gifts they'd collected, laughing at the hand-me-down clothes that had arrived at their house over the years, and modeling the silliest of them.

After a few hours, Mom looked at her watch. "Wow! It's nearly 8:00 already. Should we order a pizza?"

Camilla couldn't believe how late it was. She looked at her mom—who was wearing dusty overalls, five strands of Aunt Edna's old beads, and Granny's wide-brimmed Sunday bonnet— and couldn't help but laugh out loud. This was the best Friday night she could remember.

What is the theme of the story?
  a. Memories are a special part of life.
  b. It is important to get rid of old items.
  c. Families should spend weekends together.
  d. Sometimes things turn out to be better than expected.
  e. You never know when something could come in handy.

At the beginning of the story, Camilla did not want to spend the evening helping her mom. By the end, she was having a great time. Choice **d** is the theme of this story. Some of the other answer choices represent ideas that were presented in the story, but the underlying message that the author wanted to portray is that things can turn out to be more fun than we think they will be.

Synthesis

Suppose you were doing a research paper. You would select a topic, then to be sure you learned as much as possible, you would search a variety of texts to find information about that topic. After reading each of your sources, you would put together all the information you learned. This combination of information would provide a clear understanding of the subject.

As readers, there are times when we have to combine information to gain a complete understanding of the text. **Synthesis** means putting ideas from multiple sources together. Sometimes, readers synthesize information from different parts of a single text. Other times, they must put together information from more than one text.

Read the passage below.

Roger quietly walked to the shelf. He pulled his ball cap down on his head as he quickly looked at the items neatly lined up in front of him. Then, he grabbed a package of crackers, shoving it into his backpack as he hurried to the door, trying not to make any sound.

Think about what you know so far. Roger is being quiet; he grabs something off of a shelf and tries to quickly sneak out the door. What do you think is happening? Now, continue reading.

Roger's mom heard him opening the front door. She put the sleeping baby in her cradle, then hurried to see her son. "Honey, did you find something in the pantry to take for a snack?"

"Yeah, Mom," Roger replied. "I found the peanut butter crackers and grabbed a package. Those are my favorites. Thanks for getting them."

"Do you want me to drive you to baseball practice so you're not late?" Mom asked.

"No, I don't want you to wake Amy. I know she hasn't been sleeping much lately."

"You're a good big brother and a great son. Be careful."

Did this new information change your mind about what was happening? You may have thought Roger was being sneaky or doing something he should not have been doing. When you synthesize the new information, you gain a deeper understanding of the situation. Roger is being quiet so he doesn't wake up his sister, he's taking crackers that his mom bought for him off of a shelf in the pantry, and he's in a hurry to get to practice.

When you synthesize information, ask yourself:

- Why is this new information relevant?
- Why was the new information given?
- How does it relate to the first part of the passage?
- How does this help me gain a deeper understanding of what I've read?
- In what ways does the new information change my ideas about the passage?

Another common type of question found on the GED Language Arts, Reading exam is an **extended synthesis** question. First, you will read a passage. Then, you will be given a question. An additional piece of information about the passage or the author will be given within the question itself. You will have to combine the new information with what you read in the text to gain a deeper understanding of the passage.

First, figure out how the new information relates to what you previously read. Then, try to determine how this information helps you understand the reading passage in a deeper or different way.

Let's try an example. Be sure to read the passage carefully so that you will be able to understand the question that follows.

The winter had been especially cold. A thick, snowy blanket had covered the landscape for what seemed like months. Each day, the stack of firewood beside the house grew visibly smaller and smaller. This concerned Ella terribly. She continued to hope that the snow would be gone before the firewood.

Ella turned away from the window and returned to her writing. Somehow, writing about summer made the house feel warmer. Feeling the sun's bright rays on her face, walking barefoot in the green grass, fishing with her family, swimming in the refreshing water—these were things Ella dreamed and wrote of during the long winter months.

Here's an extended synthesis question:

The author of the passage lived during the nineteenth century in the midwestern United States. Based on the information in the story, as well as knowing the information about the author, which of the following best explains Ella's concern over the firewood?
   a. Most nineteenth century homes had large fireplaces.
   b. There was not much firewood available during the 1800s.
   c. Winters in the midwestern United States are extremely cold.
   d. Before electricity, people depended on firewood for heat and cooking.
   e. She lived in a part of the country that used more firewood than other regions.

Keep in mind that to correctly answer this question, you need to combine the information in the passage with the new information given in the question. Several answer choices could make sense. For example, it is true that many nineteenth-century homes had fireplaces and that winters in parts of the United States can be very cold. However, these facts do not consider the pieces of information that you need to synthesize.

From reading the passage, you know that Ella needs firewood. After learning the time period during which she lived, you are able to see how important firewood was for her survival. During the nineteenth century, homes did not have electricity. People had to have firewood to warm their homes and cook their meals. Choice **d** best synthesizes the information from both sources.

Let's try another example. Read the passage carefully, then read the question. Determine how the information in the question is related to the passage.

As the real estate agent walked up to the home, she admired her own photo on the "For Sale" sign in the front yard. She was anxious to get this home sold. Once inside with the homeowners, she explained the next step in selling their house.

"Your beautiful home has been on the market for several weeks now without any offers. We need to consider our options. The carpet is definitely a little bit worn in one bedroom, the bathroom wallpaper is a bit out of date, and the front yard could use some new flowers. These issues could be deterring potential buyers. I think it is time we lower the price of your home by at least 15%, if you want to get it sold."

The real estate agent will qualify for a large bonus if she sells one more house within the next month. Which of the following best describes the agent's motives in the passage?

- **a.** Her first concern is selling the house quickly so she can get the bonus.
- **b.** Her profit depends on the house selling for the highest possible price.
- **c.** She knows it is best for the owners to get the best price for their home.
- **d.** Her clients' home is currently overpriced for the neighborhood.
- **e.** She believes that home improvements are necessary for the sale of the house.

Based on the information in the passage, we do not know whether the home is overpriced, so choice **d** is incorrect. Choices **b**, **c**, and **e** may be true. However, these do not take into consideration the additional information provided within the question. This information lets us know that if the house sells quickly, the agent will receive a large bonus. When added to the information in the passage that states that she wants to lower the price of the house, we can figure out that her motivation for dropping the price is to sell the house quickly so that she can get the bonus. So, the correct answer is choice **a**.

TIP

Remember to carefully read the extended synthesis questions. Look for the additional information within the question and think about how this information relates to the passage. The information is there for a reason. You will be expected to use it as you consider your answer.

Make Connections

To better comprehend text, it is important for readers to **make connections** between what they are reading and what they already know. Not only does this help readers gain insight, but it also helps to make the material more personal and relevant. This gives readers a deeper understanding of what they read.

There are three main types of connections that great readers make:

1. text-to-self
2. text-to-text
3. text-to-world

The connections readers make are neither correct nor incorrect. The same text may remind different readers of very different things. Connections with texts are personal, and they will mean different things to different readers. The important thing is that readers connect with the text in a way that makes it meaningful and understandable to them.

Text-to-Self

Connections that readers make between the reading material and their own personal experiences are **text-to-self** connections. These make the reading more personal. Statements that could help you make such connections include the following:

- This reminds me of when I . . .
- If I were this character, I would . . .
- If this ever happened to me, I might . . .

Think about the story we read about Camilla and the garage sale. Perhaps it reminded you of a garage sale you had, of a time you came across sentimental items, or of a situation in which time flew by with your family. These would be text-to-self connections.

Text-to-Text

Text-to-text connections occur when readers are able to make connections between the reading material and a text that they have previously read. To make such connections, think about whether the text reminds you of any of the following:

- a different book by the same author
- a book with similar characters, settings, or plots
- a book that includes similar situations or events
- a book about a similar topic
- information you read in a textbook, newspaper, or magazine

Did Camilla's story remind you of another character who reconnected with his or her mom? Have you ever read an article about having a garage sale? Can you think of a book about discovering your family history? If so, these would be examples of text-to-text connections.

Text-to-World

Connections that readers make between the reading material and something that happens in the real world are **text-to-world** connections. To make this type of connection, think about whether the text reminds you of:

- information you read on the Internet
- something you saw on TV or heard on the radio
- events that are happening in the real world

If you connected Camilla's story to a television documentary on relationships between parents and teenagers or if it reminded you that there is a garage sale happening in your neighborhood this weekend, you made a text-to-world connection.

Quiz

Now that you've had a chance to review some of the skills needed to comprehend reading passages.

TIP

Notice that the first question following each passage is a purpose question, which is meant to give you a reason for reading the text. You will not be required to answer this question. Use the question to help you determine which ideas in the text deserve the most attention.

Directions: Read the following passages and choose the *one best answer* to each question.

Questions 1 through 5 refer to the following passage.

What Will Happen with the Painting?
After hours of rummaging through the various items that had been donated to the charity over the weekend, Natasha was ready to head home for the day. She had sorted the
(5) clothing, books, toys, housewares, and sporting goods into the appropriate bins and would tackle the task of pricing the items in the morning. With any luck, the items would find their place on the store shelves by
(10) tomorrow afternoon and be sold quickly.

As she turned to lock the door to the storeroom, Natasha noticed a framed canvas leaning against the wall. She wondered where it had come from and why she hadn't
(15) noticed it before now. She bent over to examine the artwork and was amazed at the bold colors and brushstrokes of the oil painting and the detail in the carved wooden frame. At the bottom corner of the
(20) piece, she noticed the signature of a world-famous artist. Amazed, she stared at the painting wondering if it was authentic or a fake. Natasha carefully traced the frame with her finger, looking for any imperfections. She
(25) couldn't help but wonder why someone would part with such a beautiful, and possibly valuable, piece of art. She carefully covered the painting with a sheet and placed it in a closet where it would be safe.

(30) Natasha could not stop thinking about the painting. Her mind was filled with questions that kept her awake most of the night. Where had it come from? Was it really the work of a famous artist? Why would
(35) someone give away a piece of art that could potentially be worth thousands of dollars? Finally, she got out of bed and went to the computer. She found the name of an art history professor at the nearby university.
(40) Maybe some of Natasha's questions would finally be answered.

1. Which is most likely the author's purpose for writing this passage?
   a. to tell readers a true story
   b. to inform readers about art history
   c. to entertain readers with a fiction tale
   d. to teach readers about a famous artist
   e. to persuade readers to donate to charity

2. Which is the meaning of the word *authentic* in line 22?
   a. old
   b. genuine
   c. famous
   d. beautiful
   e. counterfeit

3. Read the following sentence from the second paragraph:

Natasha carefully traced the frame with her finger, looking for any imperfections.

What is the meaning of *imperfection*?
a. perfect
b. improvement
c. type of disease
d. without blemish
e. a flaw or defect

4. Which statement is an example of a text-to-world connection readers might make with the passage?
a. I remember when I found a high-fashion coat at a garage sale for only $5.
b. Art appreciation has been on the rise in major cities.
c. I need to clean out my attic and donate what I find to charity.
d. An art history book I read mentioned that people sometimes don't realize they own valuable pieces of art.
e. This story reminds me of a mystery novel I read as a child about a missing painting.

5. Natasha spent many years working in an art museum and has a keen eye for valuable oil paintings. The charity she now volunteers with donates money to the local children's hospital, which is known for its impressive research program. Which sentence most accurately describes Natasha?
a. She has a large art collection that she hopes to expand.
b. She plans to return to the university and teach about art.
c. She is generous and genuinely cares about helping others.
d. She hopes to work in the field of medicine or research someday.
e. She wants to know as much as possible about the charity's donations.

Questions 6 through 10 refer to the following passage.

Will Others Change Their Minds?
Since I was a boy, it has been difficult to make friends. Many assumed that all aristocrats thought themselves better than others, but that was not the case. I never (5) believed that being a member of the highest social class made me more important than anyone.

In the streets, people stepped far out of my way, as if trying to avoid me. I smiled and (10) tried to make eye contact, but no one would meet my gaze. Groups of friends gathered on street corners and in cafes, laughing together. Loneliness filled my heart, and I longed to be a part of one of their groups. Yet somehow, I (15) would be excluded by circumstances that many would call fortunate.

One day, I stopped at the farmers' market in town to buy a piece of fruit. As I paid the gentleman, a woman sneered and (20) said, "Don't you have servants to do your shopping for you?" Several other customers

giggled and turned their backs. Smiling
politely, I thanked the man for the fruit and
walked away, listening to the whispers
(25)   behind me.

At I walked away, I noticed a young boy
sitting alone beside the bakery. He was
crying, and many people walked past him
without stopping. I sat down beside him on
(30)   the ground and asked why he was upset.

"I can't find my mother. I stopped to
look in the window of the bakery. When I
turned back around, she was gone," the boy
explained.

(35)   I put my arm around him, explaining
that he was wise to stay in one place so that
his mother could find him. "You must feel
lonely," I said. "I feel lonely, too, sometimes.
We'll stay here together until your mother
(40)   returns."

Very soon, a frantic young woman
came running down the street, calling out,
"William! William, where are you?"

The boy jumped up, and his mother
(45)   ran to us and scooped up her son in her
arms, asking if he had been afraid.

"No, Mama," William explained. "This
man kept me company."

The woman looked at me and seemed
(50)   surprised, then smiled warmly and thanked
me. William gave me a hug, then walked
away, hand in hand with his mother. As they
walked away, I realized a crowd had gathered
to watch the commotion. One person in the
(55)   crowd smiled at me, then another, then
another. For the first time, I no longer felt
like a lonely outsider.

6. Which sentence from the passage reveals its
point of view?
   a. I smiled and tried to make eye contact, but
   no one would meet my gaze.
   b. Groups of friends gathered on street corners
   and in cafes, laughing together.
   c. "Don't you have servants to do your
   shopping for you?"
   d. He was crying, and many people walked past
   him without stopping.
   e. "When I turned back around, she was gone,"
   the boy explained.

7. Considering the point of view from which the
story is told, which of the following is true?
   a. The narrator is not one of the characters in
   the story.
   b. The narrator knows the motivations of all
   the characters in the story.
   c. Readers will only know the thoughts and
   feelings of one character.
   d. Readers will know the thoughts and feelings
   of all the characters.
   e. The narrator will use pronouns such as *he* or
   she to discuss the main character.

8. Reread the first paragraph. Which would best
describe someone who is an *aristocrat*?
   a. friendly
   b. gloomy
   c. helpful
   d. lonely
   e. wealthy

9. Which statement is an example of a text-to-self connection that readers might make with the passage?

    a. It was hard for me to make friends after I moved to a new town, and for a while, I felt like an outsider.

    b. Farmers' markets are growing in popularity.

    c. There was a missing child on the news last night, but he was found this morning, safe and sound.

    d. Our social studies book talks about class conflict throughout history.

    e. I read a book called *Aristocrats* once.

10. What is the theme of the story?

    a. Friendship is a necessary part of life.

    b. It is difficult to find happiness without having great wealth.

    c. Even young children are able to make a difference in the world.

    d. Helping others is the responsibility of all members of society.

    e. It is important not to judge people before getting to know them.

Answers

1. c. This passage was written to entertain. It is not a true story, and although art history and a famous artist are mentioned, the author did not intend to teach readers about these topics. While donations to charity are mentioned, the author does not try to convince readers to make donations.

2. b. The passage tells us that Natasha wondered if the painting was "authentic or a fake." *Fake* is given as an antonym of *authentic*. So, *authentic* means *real*, or *genuine*.

3. e. The root of *imperfections* is *perfect*. The prefix *im-* means "not," so *imperfections* cause something to be not perfect. An *imperfection* is a flaw or defect that makes something not perfect. If you thought the answer was *perfect*, you selected the root of the word. If you chose "a type of disease," you may have confused the word with *infection*.

4. b. Choices **a** and **c** are examples of text-to-self connections because they relate ideas from the passage to something personal. Choices **d** and **e** make connections between the passage and other texts that have been read previously, so they are examples of text-to-text connections. Choice **b**, making a connection between the passage and something happening in the world, is a text-to-world connection.

5. c. This is an example of an expanded synthesis question. To answer it correctly, you must combine the information given in the question with what you read in the passage. Because Natasha used to work in a museum and recognizes valuable oil paintings, she probably had a pretty good idea that the artwork was worth a lot of money. The charity that now has the painting donates its money to the children's hospital, which uses some of the money for research. Natasha was obviously excited about the painting being given to the charity, which is probably because the money it raises will be given to the hospital. If she is so excited, she must really care about the people who will benefit from the donation.

6. a. This passage was written from the first-person point of view. The narrator is one of the characters in the story, and he uses pronouns such as *I* and *me*. Notice that it sounds as if the narrator is talking directly to the reader. Choice **e** also includes the pronoun *I*, but this is used in a quote by one of the other characters as he is talking to the narrator, so it does not help reveal the point of view of the passage.

7. c. Because the story tells a first-person account of the events, only the narrator's thoughts and feelings will be revealed to the readers. The narrator is a character in the story, and he only knows his own ideas and motivations, unless the other characters reveal their thoughts and feelings to him.

8. e. Context clues in the first paragraph explain that an *aristocrat* is "a member of the highest social class." Generally, people in this class have a lot of money. In this story, the aristocrat was also friendly, helpful, lonely, and possibly even gloomy. However, by definition, aristocrats are usually wealthy. As you read, remember to look for context clues in the sentences surrounding the word they help to define. In this case, the word *aristocrats* is used in one sentence, and the definition or explanation is in the sentence that follows.

9. a. Choices **b** and **c** are examples of text-to-world connections because they relate ideas from the passage to real-world events. Choices **d** and **e** make connections between the passage and other texts that have been read previously, so they are examples of text-to-text connections. Choice **a**, making a connection between the passage and something personal, is a text-to-self connection.

10. e. In this passage, people made assumptions about the narrator without getting to know him. As it turned out, these assumptions were incorrect. After others saw his helpfulness and the way he cared for the little boy, they became aware of his true personality. The narrator longed for friendships and showed that he felt helping the little boy was important, but these ideas were not the overall message the author wanted to portray. Choice **b** is the opposite of what the narrator believed, as he did have great wealth but was not happy.

Review

In this chapter, you have learned several strategies to help you better comprehend reading materials:

1. Breaking unfamiliar words into word parts, such as prefixes, suffixes, and root words, can be helpful in determining a word's meaning. Thinking of words with similar roots can also help readers figure out the meaning of unknown words.

2. Context clues such as synonyms, antonyms, definitions, and examples can be helpful in figuring out the meanings of unknown words. These clues may be in the same sentence as the unfamiliar word or in the surrounding sentences and paragraph.

3. Point of view refers to who is telling the story. First-person point of view is when one of the characters tells the story and readers see the events through his or her eyes. Third-person point of view is when the story is told by a narrator who is outside of the story and does not participate in the events. However, he or she is often aware of the thoughts and feelings of all the characters.

4. Authors usually write for one of the following purposes: to entertain, to inform, or to persuade.

5. The theme of a story is the author's underlying message. Usually, these beliefs, attitudes, or perceptions are not directly stated; instead, the theme is a lesson that readers take away from the story. The words and actions of the characters, the tone, the plot, and repeated patterns in the story help to reveal the theme.

6. Synthesizing information means putting together information from multiple sources or from more than one location within a source. Combining information can help readers gain a deeper understanding of the text.

7. Making connections between the text and what they already know helps readers better understand the material. The types of connections readers make include text-to-self, text-to-text, and text-to-world.

CHAPTER

4 ▶ POETRY

CHAPTER SUMMARY
This chapter shows you the characteristics of poetry; how figurative language is used; and how authors use style, words, mood, tone, and alliteration in poetry.

Some of the questions on the GED® Language Arts, Reading test will require you to read poetry and then answer questions about the poem. In this chapter, you will review characteristics of poetry as well as comprehension skills often needed to understand this form of literature. Many of the skills reviewed in this chapter are also important in comprehending other types of texts. Keep in mind that on the GED test, you will also need to apply the comprehension skills learned in the other chapters of this book to answer the poetry questions.

Characteristics of Poetry

As you probably already know, **poetry** differs from other types of literature in several ways. Not only do poems usually look different than prose passages, but they sound different, too.

A **poem** uses words to tell a story, express emotion, and create an image in the mind of the reader. The words are arranged in phrases or short lines rather than being written in complete sentences and paragraphs. These lines are often arranged in groups, or **stanzas**.

The following characteristics are often found in poems.

- short lines, which usually begin with a capital letter
- groups of lines, or stanzas
- descriptive words
- figurative language
- a similar number or pattern of syllables in each line
- a rhythm or beat that gives the text a musical feel
- a tone that reveals the poet's feelings
- rhyming words, often at the ends of lines
- repeated sounds

Poems can be very different from one another. Keep in mind that these characteristics may not all be found within a single poem. For instance, some poems rhyme, and others do not. Some poems include figurative language, and others do not.

A poem may be very short, or it can be as long as a novel. The poetry you will find on the GED® Language Arts, Reading test may have as few as eight lines or as many as 25. To best comprehend the writing, read poems for the sense of the words, rather than line by line. In prose writing, each sentence contains a complete thought and is ended by a period. In poetry, a single thought may continue for several lines.

Stanzas

Prose writing usually includes groups of sentences arranged into paragraphs, like the sentences in this chapter. If a sentence in prose ends in the middle of a line of text, the next begins immediately, on the same line.

Poetry is different. Short lines or phrases are used rather than sentences. Stanzas are used instead of paragraphs. Stanzas are groups of lines that are set apart from the rest of the poem. Poets may or may not divide their work into stanzas.

Read the following poem. Notice the differences between poetry and prose.

The Rainbow
After the rain, its colors show
And bend across the sky.
The rainbow touches the ground below
Then reaches the clouds up high.

The spectrum of light peeks through the gray
Reminding us not to dread,
For after the storm we always say
That brighter times are ahead.

Notice that the lines of the poem are separated into two groups, each containing four lines. These groups of lines are stanzas. So, this poem contains two stanzas. Also, notice that the phrases on each line are not complete sentences. In fact, the second stanza contains four lines but only one sentence.

Notice that each line of the poem begins with a capital letter, even though the first word on the line does not begin a new sentence. This is a characteristic that is often found in poetry.

Rhythm

As you read poetry, you will notice a musical feeling that is created by the pattern of stressed syllables in the words. This beat, or **rhythm**, is one of the distinguishing characteristics of poetry. The rhythm adds to the feeling of the piece. For example, if every second syllable is stressed, the rhythm will bounce and give the poem an upbeat feeling.

TIP

If you have trouble feeling the rhythm of a poem, try reading it aloud.

You have probably heard the following poem many times. Now, as you read it, listen to the rhythm.

One, two
Buckle my shoe.
Three, four
Shut the door.
Five, six
Pick up sticks.
Seven, eight
Lay them straight.
Nine, ten
A big fat hen.

What did you notice about the rhythm? The stressed syllables create a lively beat and suggest a lighthearted, happy feeling. The lines in a poem usually have a similar number or pattern of beats. Each line of this poem has between two and four beats.

Now, read the following poem and think about how the rhythm is different than that of "One, Two / Buckle my shoe."

After sleeping in the chrysalis
Withdrawn from the outside world
The beautiful butterfly emerges
With its newly formed wings unfurled.

You probably noticed that the slower rhythm gives a calmer feeling. Poets use rhythm to help create the feelings they want the readers to have when reading their work.

Rhyme

You already know that when words **rhyme** they have the same ending sound, such as *string* and *thing*. Many poems contain rhyming words, or words with similar sounds, at the ends of lines.

One, two
Buckle my shoe.
Three, four
Shut the door.

In this part of the poem, *two* and *shoe* are rhyming words. *Four* and *door* also rhyme.

Not all poems rhyme. However, when they do, the poem usually has a **rhyme scheme**, or a pattern that explains how the rhyming words are arranged. The first line is labeled *A*. Any words that rhyme with the word at the end of the line are also considered *A*. The word at the end of the next line is labeled *A* if it rhymes with the first line. If not, it is labeled *B*. Any words that rhyme with the word at the end of line *B* are given the same label, and so on.

Let's figure out the rhyme scheme of this poem.

One, <u>two</u> (A)
Buckle my <u>shoe</u>. (A)
Three, <u>four</u> (B)
Shut the <u>door</u>. (B)

Two is the word at the end of the first line, so we'll call that line *A*. Since *shoe* rhymes with *two*, the second line is also *A*. *Four* does not rhyme with *two* and *shoe*, so it is given the next letter, *B*. Because *door* rhymes with *four*, that line is also *B*. So, the rhyme scheme of these lines is AABB.

Now you try it. What is the rhyme scheme of the following poem? Write your answer on the line underneath it.

Roses are red,
Violets are blue,

Sugar is sweet,
And so are you.

You probably noticed that nothing rhymes with the first line, lines two and four rhyme, and nothing rhymes with the third line. So, the rhyme scheme of this poem is ABCB.

Look back at "The Rainbow," the poem at the beginning of the chapter. What rhyme scheme do you notice in these stanzas?

Each stanza contains two pairs of rhyming words. In each stanza, alternating lines rhyme: lines one and three rhyme, and lines two and four rhyme. So, the rhyme scheme is ABAB CDCD.

Figurative Language

Without even realizing it, you probably use both literal and figurative language every day. **Literal language** refers to words that state a factual meaning. **Figurative language** is when words have a meaning that is different than their literal meaning.

The captain and his crew were in the same boat for three days.

This is an example of literal language. These people are actually in a boat together.

Raul and his classmates were in the same boat when the teacher gave the pop quiz.

In this case, there is not an actual boat. The phrase *in the same boat* is a type of figurative language meaning

that they were facing the same situation. This is an example of an idiom. Idioms are explained later in this chapter.

As you read both poetry and prose, look for the types of figurative language in the following list:

- similes
- metaphors
- personification
- hyperbole
- idioms

Don't worry if you are unfamiliar with any of these terms, as they are all covered in this chapter.

Writers often use figurative language to make their writing more interesting, create images in the minds of the readers, and help readers better comprehend the text. Because of its descriptive nature, figurative language is often found in poetry. Recognizing and understanding the language used can help you gain a better understanding of what you read.

Similes

Have you ever heard someone say "He was as quiet as a mouse"? This is an example of a simile. A **simile** is a type of figurative language that uses the word *like* or *as* to compare two things. Similes are often used to create a clear picture of the person or object being described.

Meredith's face was as white as a ghost.

This comparison is used to explain exactly how white Meredith's face was. She may not have actually been the same color as a ghost, but the simile effectively paints a picture of how she looked.

The track star could run like the wind.

Was the track star actually as fast as the wind? Probably not. But the comparison lets readers know that he or she could run very quickly. That's more interesting than saying, "The athlete could run really fast," isn't it?

Keep in mind that not every sentence that contains the words *like* or *as* is a simile. To be a simile, the phrase must make a comparison.

> *Mr. Gonzalez enjoys his career as an attorney.*
>
> *Erin slept like a baby after gymnastics practice.*
>
> *We would like to see the movie on opening weekend.*

All three of these sentences use either the word *like* or *as*. Can you tell which one is a simile? The second sentence uses the word *like* to compare how Erin slept to the way a baby sleeps. This simile is used to show how restful she was.

Now you try it. What is the meaning of the following simile?

> *Viktor painted the election poster like an artist putting the finishing touches on a masterpiece.*

An artist would be extremely careful when putting the finishing touches on a masterpiece and would take the work very seriously. This simile shows the care, thought, and effort Viktor put into creating his poster.

Metaphors

Metaphors compare two things by stating that one object *is* another. These comparisons are different from similes in that they do not include the words *like* or *as*.

> *The news anchorman's face was stony while he read the updated report.*

This metaphor makes a comparison by stating that his face was stony. The comparison gives the clear picture that his face did not move or smile during this time.

> *Our English classroom was a refrigerator this afternoon.*

To figure out the meaning of a metaphor, first identify the two things that are being compared. In this case, the classroom and a refrigerator are the objects of the comparison. Then, determine how the two might be similar. Because we know that a refrigerator is very cold, this figure of speech points out that the classroom was also very cold.

This simple metaphor actually portrays quite a bit of information. It lets readers know that the classroom was more than just a bit chilly; it was probably so cold that the temperature felt uncomfortable. The writer was able to use a metaphor to share quite a bit of information and give readers a clear understanding of the information he was trying to convey. Also, the metaphor was much more interesting than simply saying, "The classroom sure was cold today."

Personification

Personification is a type of figurative language that gives human characteristics to nonhuman things to give readers a more clear description.

> *The sailboat crawled across the horizon.*

This description paints a clear picture of how the sailboat moved, although crawling is something that humans do, not sailboats.

> *The gentle wind whispered in the trees.*

To recognize personification, ask yourself, *What nonhuman object is given a human characteristic?* In this case, *wind* is the nonhuman thing, and *whispered* is the human characteristic attributed to it.

As you read the next poem, look for examples of personification. Write these examples of figurative language on the lines underneath the poem.

Its branches reaching toward the sky,
Leaves dancing in the wind,
The tall tree stands, then bows a bit
As it welcomes the sun again.

_____

_____

There are several examples of personification in this poem. You probably recognized *branches reaching; leaves dancing; tall tree stands, then bows;* and the tree *welcomes the sun.* These verbs are usually actions performed by humans. Nonhuman things do not *reach, dance, bow,* or *welcome.* However, the poet uses these descriptions to help readers visualize the actions in the poem.

Hyperbole

You've probably used hyperbole a million times without even realizing what it is. In fact, you just read an example of this type of figurative language in the previous sentence. **Hyperbole** is an exaggeration that is used for emphasis or effect. In all reality, you probably have used hyperbole before but not actually a million times.

Garrison was so hungry he could eat a horse.

When she is angry, Celeste talks a mile a minute.

Terrell's attitude is bigger than the state of Texas.

Each of these sentences contains an example of hyperbole. The exaggerations are obvious, but they give the reader a clear idea of what is being described. From these examples, we know that Garrison is terribly hungry, Celeste can talk extremely quickly, and Terrell has quite an attitude.

See whether you can recognize the hyperbole in the following sentence.

Natasha jumped 50 feet in the air when she saw the mouse scurry across the kitchen floor.

What does the hyperbole in the sentence tell you?
a. The mouse ran quickly.
b. Natasha has a pet mouse.
c. Natasha jumped very high.
d. The kitchen has a high ceiling.
e. The mouse was afraid of Natasha.

Natasha jumped 50 feet in the air is an exaggeration used to emphasize the fact that she jumped very high (choice **c**). The figurative language is used as an interesting type of description that helps the reader understand what happened when Natasha saw the mouse.

Idioms

Sometimes a phrase can have different meanings, depending on the situation in which the words are used.

Those concert tickets cost an arm and a leg!

Well, people who do purchase the tickets won't have to attend the event without two of their limbs. **Idioms** are expressions that have a different meaning than what the words literally indicate. To say that something *cost an arm and a leg* simply means that it was expensive.

Ms. Chester ate a piece of cake for dessert.

Our English quiz was a piece of cake!

How is the meaning of the underlined phrase different in each sentence?

_____

_____

The first sentence uses the literal meaning of the words "piece of cake"; Ms. Chester ate some cake at the end of a meal. The second sentence uses the figurative meaning of the words. In this idiom, "piece of cake" means that something was very easy.

Here are a few common idioms that you have probably heard before:

- over the moon
- hold your horses
- wet behind the ears
- have your hands full
- beat around the bush
- something up his sleeve

Look for examples of figurative language as you read the following poem.

> The alarm clock screamed this morning,
> My room was as black as night.
> Thunder cracked as lightning snapped
> And filled my heart with fright!
>
> I opened up my window
> And carefully stuck out my head.
> It was raining cats and dogs out there,
> So I just stayed in bed.

List the examples of figurative language in the poem on the following lines. Tell what type of figurative language each represents as well as its meaning.

_____

_____

_____

_____

The poem had three examples of figurative language. Did you find all of them? *The alarm clock screamed* is an example of personification. This comparison shows that the sound of the clock was loud and piercing, like a person's scream. *As black as night* is a simile explaining just how dark it was outside. And *raining cats and dogs* is an idiom that means it was raining really hard that morning. You could also say that *raining cats and dogs* is hyperbole, meaning that it is an exaggeration of how much rain was actually falling. Whether you call it an idiom or hyperbole, it's still figurative language.

Style

When you think about the word *style*, you probably think about someone's clothes or a person's overall look. In many ways, someone's style is a way to reveal his or her personality. A friend who always wears T-shirts and flip-flops has a casual style and maybe a laid-back personality. A woman who always wears dark-colored dresses with high heels and pearls has a professional style and maybe a more formal personality.

Writers have personalities, too. The type of language used to express ideas forms the **style** of the passage. The following three types of styles are often found in writing:

1. formal
2. informal
3. conversational

Different writing styles are appropriate in different situations, much like different clothing styles are suitable in different situations. For example, if you were going to a ball game, you'd likely throw on a pair of shorts, some sneakers, a T-shirt, and a hat. This style is perfectly acceptable for sitting on the sidelines. However, it would not be appropriate for a religious service, job interview, or opera.

Consider the style of writing you use to send an e-mail or text to your best friend. Would you use that same style to fill out a resume for a job or to complete a term paper? Probably not, if you actually hope to get the job or earn a good grade on your paper.

Formal Style

A **formal style** is appropriate for research reports, legal or workplace documents, and technical articles. The audience for such writing usually consists of experts in a given field, so the writing may include complicated words and technical jargon. Such writing may be difficult to comprehend at times.

After reviewing the most recent research, the management team of our company unanimously agreed that alterations to the machinery could negatively impact the production rates in our factories and ultimately decrease our profitability.

As you read passages with a formal style, you may notice that the writing has a professional or proper feel.

Informal Style

An **informal style** is often found in magazines, newspapers, and books that are intended for the general public. The words are familiar and simple enough that most people would easily be able to understand the writing.

Tuesday, the mayor gave a speech at Washington Middle School. Afterward, she spent nearly half an hour answering students' questions. She seemed happy that so many young people wanted to learn about their community.

Notice that the words and information in the passage would be easily understood by nearly all readers.

Conversational Style

The least formal type of writing uses a **conversational style**. This writing includes words and phrases that people use when speaking. The words are common and easy to understand and may include slang expressions.

You won't believe what happened when I got home today! There was a huge box on the porch from my aunt. I ripped it open, and she had sent me the most awesome striped shirt ever! My aunt totally rocks!

When you read this type of writing, you can almost hear a friend saying the words to you. It sounds like a conversation.

Let's practice what you've learned about style. Read the following passage and determine whether the writer used a formal, informal, or conversational style.

This Saturday, the Greater Bay Aquarium will be holding its annual fundraising event. There will be a silent auction, a bake sale, and carnival games. All proceeds will be used to build a new dolphin pool. Admission to the event is free, but donations are always welcome.

Think about the type of words used and the sound of the text. What is the style of this passage?

_____

You probably noticed that the writer included familiar words and that the information was written in such a way that it would be easily understood by the general public. The writer used an informal style.

Had the writer used a formal style, more difficult words would have been included, and you probably would have noticed a more serious feeling to the passage. The following sentence is an example of what you might have found in the paragraph if it had used a formal style:

Aquatic mammals, such as the dolphin, require larger habitats than those currently provided by this facility.

The writer could have chosen to use a conversational style, in which case you might have found sentences similar to this example:

Look at those dolphins. They are the neatest animals! Do you know what these guys need? A bigger pool! The folks here at the aquarium would love to give them the kind of home they deserve. Come on over to the fundraiser this weekend and help us out. It's sure to be a blast!

Word Usage

As mentioned in the previous section, the words an author chooses help determine the style of a passage. Regardless of whether the passage is poetry or prose, writers carefully select the words that are included in their work. **Word usage** refers to the words chosen by writers to represent their ideas, express their attitudes, share information, set the tone of the piece, and draw forth the desired response from readers. This is also sometimes referred to as **diction**.

The customer <u>asked</u> to speak with the store manager.

The customer <u>demanded</u> to speak with the store manager.

The only difference between these two sentences is a single word, yet they convey very different attitudes. In the first sentence, readers might assume that the customer was pleasant. In the second sentence, the word *demanded* implies that the customer was angry and insistent.

The driver <u>said</u> the light was green when he entered the intersection.

The driver <u>claimed</u> the light was green when he entered the intersection.

Again, only one word is different in these sentences. However, the word *claimed* in the second sentence reveals the author's attitude about the situation. The author does not state that he doesn't believe the driver; however, his disbelief is implied.

Word usage and figurative language often work together to create the emotions or express the attitudes the writer wants to share with the audience. Think about the difference between the comparisons *It was as sharp as a tack* and *It was as sharp as a dagger*. Both similes express how sharp the item was, but the word *dagger* creates a more serious, almost scary feeling. Think about how the following are different: *He moved as smoothly as an ice skater, gliding across a frozen pond* and *He moved as smoothly as a cobra, slithering through the tall grass*. In both cases, word usage shows how he moved, but the different similes leave readers with different feelings and impressions about what was taking place.

As you know, many words have more than one meaning. Writers often use such words, but the most familiar meaning might not be the intended one. Chapter 3 reviewed the use of context clues—such as synonyms, antonyms, definitions, and examples—to determine the meanings of words. Sometimes these hints are not included in the text. You will need to think carefully about which meaning is correct, depending on how the word is used in the passage. Understanding word usage is important in fully understanding the meaning of a passage.

Melissa lost her necklace when the clasp broke.

The use of the word *clasp* in the sentence indicates that it is a small fastener that holds jewelry together. Another meaning for this word is to hold something, as in the next sentence.

The little girl knew she needed to clasp her mother's hand to cross the street.

Word usage indicates which meaning of the word *clasp* the author intends to use. Understanding that the way a word is used can impact its meaning is an important strategy in understanding text.

Mr. Chang told Ty not to badger his brother.

The ranger saw a badger run through the forest.

Notice how the usage of the word *badger* determines its meaning in these sentences. In fact, it is a verb in the first example, and a noun in the second. Be sure to read sentences carefully to determine which of a word's meanings the author intends to depict.

Now it's your turn. Think about what we've reviewed about word usage to answer the question.

Every day after school, Kelly goes to the barn to groom her horse.

What is the meaning of the word *groom* in the preceding sentence?
a. a man who is getting married
b. someone who cares for horses
c. an officer in a royal household
d. to care for an animal's appearance
e. to train someone for a particular job

Notice that in the sentence, *groom* is used as a verb. Although answer b refers to horses, this meaning is a noun, so it is not the correct choice. Neither is a or c, for the same reason. (Other reasons are that Kelly is not going to the barn to get married and is not an officer in a royal household.)

To determine which meaning the author has in mind, pay close attention to how the word is used in the sentence. While answer choice e is a verb, Kelly is not training anyone for a job in this sentence. The correct answer is d, which uses the word *groom* as a verb meaning to take care of an animal's appearance.

Mood and Tone

Not only do the words an author chooses represent his or her ideas, they also help to set the tone, or mood, of the story. The **mood** refers to the feelings or emotions that the text gives to the readers. The words, details, setting, and dialogue used in a passage might suggest different attitudes or emotions—such as happiness, anger, or humor—and let readers know how the author feels about the topic.

The living room was full of people chatting and filling the air with laughter.

The author's description of the situation suggests a feeling of happiness. Everyone seems to be having a good time, and the reader is probably content.

The living room was crowded and noisy, with rude people talking over one another.

This description explains the same situation in a much different way. It may leave readers with an uncomfortable or irritated feeling. A writer chooses words that will evoke the feelings, emotions, and mood he or she wants to create.

The hostess had expected a large crowd. She sat down, alone, and stared at the long table full of food before her. With a sigh, she leaned over and blew out the candles.

What is the mood of the passage?

_____

This passage probably draws forth feelings of sadness or loneliness. The hostess had not expected to be by herself and appears to be disappointed at the lack of guests. As you read, think about which words stir up emotions. These may be good clues about the mood of the passage.

Have you ever heard the saying "It's not what you say, but how you say it"? A lot can be revealed by the way you share information. Often, how you say something tells a lot about your feelings or attitude toward the subject.

Writers also use words and details to share their attitudes about a topic. This attitude is referred to as the **tone** of a passage. The tone might be humorous, sarcastic, angry, excited, formal, or playful, just to list a few. The tone often goes hand in hand with the author's purpose. For example, a piece that is written to inform might have a more formal, serious tone. A piece that is written to entertain may be humorous and include conversational or informal language.

The smells wafting in from the kitchen were aromatic.

What do you think the author's attitude was toward the smells coming from the kitchen? *Aromatic* is definitely a word that suggests a positive attitude or tone.

For the entire night, we were subjected to the deafening sounds of the band practicing next door.

The tone of this sentence definitely shares the writer's attitude about the band's practice. *Subjected to* and *deafening* suggest an angry, negative, or outraged tone.

Notice that the tone gives clues about the writer's feelings. The same is true when you talk with others. Their tone of voice often tells you how they feel. Mood and tone often work together. Keep this in mind as you read and interpret texts.

TIP

The way sentences are written may offer clues about the tone of a piece. For example, short, choppy sentences or phrases can suggest excitement or maybe anger. Longer, flowing sentences may suggest happiness or a peaceful tone.

Read the excerpt of the poem by William Blake. As you read, look for clues about the tone of the poem.

Spring

Sound the flute!
Now it's mute.
Birds' delight,
Day and night.
Nightingale
In the dale.
Lark in sky
Merrily,
Merrily, merrily to welcome in the year.

What is the tone of the poem?

_____

You probably determined that the tone of the poem is happy, joyous, or carefree. Words and phrases such as *Birds' delight* and *merrily* are clues about the poet's feelings and attitudes toward spring.

Alliteration

One strategy writers use to emphasize words or to connect words and ideas is alliteration. **Alliteration** is the repetition of sounds in a group of words. These repeated sounds are usually found at the beginning of words; however, the repeated sound may also begin a stressed syllable found within a word. There are two types of alliteration:

- **Assonance** is the repetition of vowel sounds.
- **Consonance** is the repetition of consonant sounds.

> *With butterflies dancing in the wind,*
> *Fairies flitting fearlessly on air,*
> *The easy breeze floats away*
> *Without a single care.*

This poem contains two examples of alliteration. *Fairies flitting fearlessly* is an example of consonance. Each of these words begins with the same consonant sound. *Easy breeze* repeats the same vowel sounds and is an example of assonance. Notice that the repeated sound is at the beginning of the first word and in the middle of the second.

> *Across the canyon, cascading beams of sun . . .*

The phrase is another example of consonance. The repeated sound begins the stressed syllable in *across* and is found at the beginning of *canyon* and *cascading*.

By definition, alliteration is the repetition of sounds, not the repetition of letters. The same sound could be spelled with different letters. For example, *gentle* and *jumping* begin with different letters but the same sound.

> *Spiders cease to spin their webs.*

Spiders, *cease*, and *spin* all begin with the same repeated sound. However, they do not all begin with the same letter.

> *Grass moves gently in the breeze.*

Grass and *gently* both begin with the same letter, but they do not begin with the same sound. *Gently* begins with the same sound as *justice*. So, despite the fact that the same letters are repeated, this is not an example of alliteration because the same sounds are not repeated.

What examples of alliteration are found in the following poem? Underline the repeated sounds and on the following lines, tell whether they represent assonance or consonance.

> *He sees the rain each evening*
> *As it falls onto the lawn,*
> *And watches water glisten*
> *As dewdrops dance again at dawn.*

_____

_____

He, *sees*, *each*, and *evening* represent a repeated vowel sound and are an example of assonance. *Fall* and *lawn* also have the same vowel sound. Assonance and consonance are both found in the words *watches* and *water*. *Dewdrops*, *dance*, and *dawn* repeat the same consonant sound. These are an example of consonance. Notice that *dewdrops* repeats the sound twice within the same word.

Quiz

Now that you've had a chance to review some of the skills needed to comprehend poetry, give the following questions a try.

Directions: Read each poem and choose the *one best answer* to each question.

Questions 1 through 5 refer to the following poem by Emily Dickinson.

What Does the Grass Do?

The grass so little has to do,—
A sphere of simple green,
With only butterflies to brood,
And bees to entertain,

(5)   And stir all day to pretty tunes
The breezes fetch along,
And hold the sunshine in its lap
And bow to everything;

And thread the dews all night, like pearls,
(10) And make itself so fine,—
A duchess were too common
For such a noticing.
And even when it dies, to pass
In odors so divine,
(15) As lowly spices gone to sleep,
Or amulets of pine.

And then to dwell in sovereign barns,
And dream the days away, —
The grass so little has to do,
(20) I wish I were a hay!

1. Which line from the poem contains an example of a simile?
   a. 1
   b. 7
   c. 9
   d. 16
   e. 20

2. The idea that the grass has "bees to entertain" (line 4) is an example of what kind of figurative language?
   a. metaphor
   b. simile
   c. hyperbole
   d. idiom
   e. personification

3. Which is an example of consonance?
   a. With only butterflies to brood
   b. And bow to everything
   c. In odors so divine
   d. The grass so little has to do
   e. I wish I were a hay!

4. How does the poet feel about the smell of the grass?
   a. She is not fond of the smell.
   b. She thinks it smells wonderful.
   c. She finds the smell unpleasant.
   d. She believes it smells like spices.
   e. She states that it smells like pine.

5. Which word expresses the mood of the poem?
   a. complacent
   b. envious
   c. thrilled
   d. wishful
   e. worrisome

Questions 6 through 10 refer to the following poem by Robert Frost.

What Will Happen to the Branches?

I walked down alone on Sunday after church
To the place where John has been cutting trees
To see for myself about the birch
He said I could have to bush my peas.

(5) The sun in the new cut, narrow gap
Was hot enough for the first of May,
And stifling hot with the odor of sap
From stumps still bleeding their life away.

The frogs that were peeping a thousand shrill
(10) Wherever the ground was low and wet,
The minute they heard my step went still
To watch me and see what I came to get.

Birch boughs enough piled everywhere,
All fresh and sound from the recent ax.
(15) Time someone came with cart and pair
And got them off the wildflowers' backs.

They might be good for garden things
To curl a little finger round,
The same as you seize cat's cradle strings,
(20) And lift themselves up off the ground.

Small good to anything growing wild,
They were crooking many a trillium
That had budded before the boughs were piled
And since it was coming up had come.

6. How many stanzas are in the poem?
   a. 4
   b. 5
   c. 6
   d. 20
   e. 24

7. What is the rhyme scheme of each stanza in the poem?
   a. AAAB
   b. AABB
   c. ABAB
   d. ABCB
   e. ABCD

8. Which line contains an example of alliteration?
   a. 7
   b. 14
   c. 16
   d. 20
   e. 23

9. Which of these is used in an example of personification?
   a. ax
   b. boughs
   c. frogs
   d. stumps
   e. sun

10. Read the excerpt from the beginning of the poem:

I walked down alone on Sunday after church
To the place where John has been cutting trees
To see for myself about the birch
He said I could have to bush my peas.

Which is used to indicate the style of the passage?
   a. technical vocabulary
   b. common words and slang
   c. two pairs of rhyming words
   d. familiar words that are easily understood
   e. jargon that would be understood by experts

Answers

1. c. There is one example of a simile in the lines that are answer choices. It is found in line 9, where dew is being threaded *like* pearls. It could be argued that line 1 contains figurative language, but this would be a personification of the grass. Line 7, where the breeze is holding the sunshine in its lap, could also be considered personification.

2. e. Giving a nonhuman object (the grass) the ability to "entertain" is an example of personification.

3. a. The same beginning consonant sound is repeated in *butterflies* and *brood*. Choice **c** includes a repeated vowel sound in *odors* and *so*; this is an example of assonance. Choice **b** is an example of personification. Choices **d** and **e** are not examples of consonance and are thus not correct.

4. b. In line 14, the poet refers to "odors so divine." The word *divine* means "lovely" or "pleasant." Remember what we reviewed about word usage; the word *divine* was carefully selected to portray the poet's thoughts and beliefs. This would indicate that she found the smell of the grass to be pleasant, lovely, or wonderful. The poet does mention "lowly spices" and "amulets of pine" (choices **d** and **e**), but they are not the best choice to describe how the poet feels about the smell of grass.

5. d. The poet is wishing that she were like the grass. *Envious* implies a negative feeling, and although she wishes to be like the grass, the mood of the poem is positive. The other choices do not accurately describe the mood of the poem.

6. c. This poem has a total of 24 lines, which are divided into six stanzas. Each stanza has four lines.

7. c. In each stanza, the words at the ends of the first and third lines rhyme, and the words at the ends of the second and fourth lines rhyme. The first line would be labeled *A*, as would any lines that rhyme with it. The second line would be labeled *B*, as would any lines that rhyme with it. Consequently, this is an ABAB rhyme scheme.

8. e. *Budded*, *before*, and *boughs* all contain the same beginning consonant sound. This is an example of alliteration, specfically consonance.

9. d. In the poem, stumps are given the human trait of bleeding. This is used to explain how the sap was running from the freshly cut trees.

10. d. The use of familiar words and the fact that the excerpt could be easily understood by most readers indicate that the style of the passage is informal. Choices **a** and **e** would likely be found in a passage with a formal style. Answer choice **b** would be found in a passage with a conversational style. The inclusion or exclusion of rhyming words in a poem does not affect the style of the piece.

In this chapter, you learned several strategies to help you better comprehend poems as well as other types of reading materials:

1. Poems are a literary form that use words to tell a story, express emotion, and create an image in the mind of the reader.

2. Poems differ from prose in several ways:
   - Words are arranged in phrases or short lines.
   - Lines are often arranged in groups.
   - Each line usually begins with a capital letter.
   - There are a similar number of syllables, or a pattern of syllables, in each line.
   - The words at the ends of the lines may or may not rhyme.

3. Often, groups of lines in a poem are arranged together in stanzas. Each stanza is set part from the rest of the poem.

4. Poems have a rhythm, or beat, that is created by the pattern of stressed syllables in each line. The lines of a poem usually have the same, or a similar number of beats, or there may be a pattern to the number of beats in the lines. The rhythm helps create the feeling of the poem.

5. Many poems rhyme, although they do not have to. Often, rhyming words are arranged at the ends of lines. The pattern of rhyming words within a poem is the rhyme scheme.

6. Poems often include figurative language, or language that has a different meaning than the literal meaning of the words. Types of figurative language include the following:
   - similes
   - metaphors
   - personification
   - hyperbole
   - idiom

7. A simile is a comparison made between two things using the words *like* or *as*. *Aunt Betty's voice was as sweet as syrup* is an example of a simile.

8. A metaphor compares two things by stating that one object actually is the other. *The candidate was a statue as he waited to hear the results of the election* is an example of a metaphor.

9. Personification describes a nonhuman thing by giving it human traits or characteristics. *The sun winked from behind the clouds* is an example of personification.

10. Hyperbole is an intended exaggeration used for emphasis or effect. *Dylan was 10-feet tall when he was chosen as captain of the football team* is an example of hyperbole.

11. An idiom is a group of words or a phrase that has a different meaning than that of the words individually. *LaToya's mom told her to break a leg at her ballet recital* is an example of an idiom.

12. A writer's style refers to the type of words and language used to express his or her ideas. The style of a piece might be one of the following:
- formal
- informal
- conversational

13. A formal writing style includes complicated words. It can be difficult to understand at times.

14. An informal writing style uses familiar words and is easily understood by the general public.

15. A conversational writing style includes common words and slang and sounds like the writer is talking directly with readers. It is the least formal of the writing styles.

16. Word usage refers to the words a writer selects to express his or her ideas and attitudes, share information, and elicit a desired response from readers. At times, readers may have to look at how words are used to determine which of a word's meanings the writer has in mind.

17. The mood of a passage is the feeling it gives readers and is created by the words, details, setting, and dialogue of the text.

18. The tone is the writer's attitude toward the subject. The words and details reveal the tone of the text.

19. Alliteration is the repetition of sounds used to emphasize words and connect ideas.

20. Consonance is a type of alliteration that repeats consonant sounds. Assonance is a type of alliteration that repeats vowel sounds.

C H A P T E R

5 ▶ DRAMA

CHAPTER SUMMARY

This chapter tells you how a drama's script and story elements both differentiate it from and make it similar to prose. It also tells you how to connect a text to yourself, to other texts, and to the world as well as how to draw conclusions.

I f you have ever seen the performance of a play, you are sure to have noticed differences between watching the actions unfold and listening to someone read the story aloud. If you have ever read a play, you have most likely noticed differences between the way it is written and the way a typical story is written.

A **drama** is a written work that was intended to be acted out on stage. The majority of the writing consists of conversations between the characters. There are several ways in which drama and prose are similar; there are also several important differences between the two genres.

Both drama and prose:

- have a plot
- tell a story
- involve a setting
- include characters

However, drama:

- is written as a script
- is divided into acts and scenes
- is meant to be performed by actors and enjoyed by an audience
- includes stage directions

On the other hand, prose:

- is written in paragraph form
- is divided into chapters
- is meant to be enjoyed by readers

In this chapter, we review the characteristics of dramas and several comprehension strategies that can help you better understand this form of literature. Many of these strategies will come in handy when trying to grasp a deeper understanding of other types of literature as well.

The Parts of a Script

When you read a script, you will notice that it looks different than prose. It will likely include a cast list, acts, scenes, dialogue, and stage directions. Recognizing each of these and understanding their purpose will help you better comprehend the drama.

Cast List

When you read prose, the characters are usually introduced as they become involved in the story. For example, think about *Goldilocks and the Three Bears.* First, the bear family is introduced as they sit down to breakfast. Then, after they leave to go for a walk while the porridge cools down, Goldilocks enters the story. Readers meet her when she enters the bears' home.

A script introduces all of the characters before the story begins. A **cast list** is included at the beginning and introduces all the characters readers will encounter throughout the story or at least in that sec-

tion of the story. Sometimes, a short description of each character is included.

> The **cast** is the group of actors or performers in a production such as a drama or play.

If *Goldilocks and the Three Bears* had been a drama, the cast list might look something like this:

Characters

Papa Bear . . . adult bear; father of the bear family

Mama Bear . . . adult bear; mother of the bear family

Baby Bear . . . young bear cub; child of Papa Bear and Mama Bear

Goldilocks . . . young girl with golden hair, about 10 years old

If your school or another group of actors was performing this play, the cast list would include the names of the characters as well as the people performing each role.

Papa Bear . . . Jose Rodriguez

Mama Bear . . . Desiree Washington

Baby Bear . . . Ryan Costello

Goldilocks . . . Adrienne Perry

After all the characters are introduced in the cast list, the names of those appearing in specific parts of the drama may be listed at the beginning of that section of the script.

"The Porridge Problem"

(Papa Bear, Mama Bear, and Baby Bear)

Because only the bear family appears in the first section of the drama, where Mama serves the porridge, they are the only characters listed here. Goldilocks is not in this scene, so her name is not on the list.

Acts and Scenes

Long plays are often divided into major sections called **acts**. These could be compared to chapters in prose. Acts are often referred to by their sequential number, such as Act I, Act II, Act III, and so on. Often, during the performance of a play, there is an intermission between acts.

Many times, acts are divided into smaller divisions called **scenes**. A scene is a specific episode from the story, which occurs in a single place during a set period of time. Every time a new setting is introduced, a new scene begins. Often, the setting is described at the beginning of the scene. The location and the time of day are usually introduced.

> A **play** may have only a single act, or it may include a number of acts and scenes. For example, Shakespeare's *Romeo and Juliet* has five acts and a total of 24 scenes. Each time the setting changes, so does the scene. The setting for Act I, Scene 1 is a public place in Verona, Italy. Act I, Scene 2 takes place on a street. The setting changes, and Act I, Scene 3 occurs in the home of one of the main characters.

Suppose *The Three Little Pigs* were written as a script. The scene would change each time we visited a different pig's home. Scene 1 would probably take place at the house built from straw. Scene 2 would begin when the story moves to the house built with twigs, and so on. Notes at the beginning of the scene would let readers know where and when this particular part of the story happens.

Dialogue

The most important part of any drama is the dialogue. **Dialogue** refers to the words of the characters. In a play, this is what helps readers get to know the characters and what moves the story forward. Most of the story is told through the dialogue.

Many prose stories include dialogue as well, but prose also includes a narrator to explain the actions, feelings, and motives of the characters. Much of the story is told by the narrator. In a drama, readers must depend on dialogue for the majority of this information.

Another difference between the dialogue in prose and drama is the way it is written.

"What are your plans for this afternoon?" asked Mrs. Donovan.

"Laurie and I are headed to the library to study for our geometry quiz, then we have cheerleading practice," replied Tara. "I'll definitely be home in time for dinner, though."

When reading prose, words such as *asked Mrs. Donovan* and *replied Tara* indicate the speaker. Also, the characters' words are enclosed in quotation marks. Compare the same conversation with a script's dialogue:

Mrs. Donovan: *What are your plans for this afternoon?*

Tara: *Laurie and I are headed to the library to study for our geometry quiz, then we have cheerleading practice. I'll definitely be home in time for dinner, though.*

A script introduces the speaker, followed by his or her words. The name of the character is written at the beginning of the line, usually in all capital letters, followed by a colon. The words that he or she speaks are written after the colon. Notice that there are no quotation marks, and when the speaker changes, a new line begins.

Now you try it. Read the dialogue below, then rewrite it as a script on the lines provided.

"I'm so glad to see you," Kelvin said. "Where were you yesterday?"

"We went out of town for the weekend," Hailey explained. "We stayed with my aunt and uncle for a couple of days."

"That's great," replied Marisol. "Welcome back!"

_____

_____

_____

_____

_____

_____

You probably recognized that there were three different speakers in this dialogue: Kelvin, Hailey, and Marisol. Each of their names should be written in all capital letters before the words they speak, and a new line should begin each time the speaker changes. Check to make sure that your response is the same as the correct dialogue below.

Kelvin: *I'm so glad to see you. Where were you yesterday?*

Hailey: *We went out of town for the weekend. We stayed with my aunt and uncle for a couple of days.*

Marisol: *That's great. Welcome back!*

Stage Directions

Another element found in drama is the **stage directions**, which indicate the characters' actions, tone of voice, feelings, and facial expressions. These bits of information are usually found in parentheses, following the character's name.

Lucas (*raising his arms in the air and shouting angrily*): There's no way I'm taking the blame for that!

These stage directions explain the character's gestures, tone of voice, and mood. They also serve to tell actors how the lines should be read. Such information helps readers accurately understand what is happening in the drama.

Simone: *You won't believe what just happened!*

What can you tell about Simone in this line of dialogue? It's possible that she just won the student council elections and is filled with excitement. It's also possible that she just found out her best friend is moving to a new town and is devastated. Or, like Lucas in the previous example, she could be angry. A little extra information would certainly be helpful in deciphering her mood.

Simone (*running excitedly into the room, waving her report card and smiling*): You won't believe what just happened!

Now, readers know exactly how Simone is acting and feeling. Stage directions give readers a clear picture of the actions and emotions that occur along with the dialogue.

In a play that is being performed on stage, the stage directions also let the actors know when to enter and exit the stage, and they let the crew know when to do technical things, such as dim the lights or start the music.

The following terms are often found in stage directions, so it is helpful to understand them:

- stage left: the actors' left hand side when facing the audience
- stage right: the actors' right hand side when facing the audience
- center stage: the middle of the performance area

Now you try your hand at reading dialogue with stage directions. As you read, pay attention to who is speaking and what actions and emotions are occurring in the scene. After you read, answer the questions that follow.

School science lab, after class

Regan (*picking up her books and walking toward the door*): That was a tough chemistry test! I really studied hard but am still not sure I passed.

Aaron (*shaking his head slowly*): Me either. Science is usually my best subject, but wow!

Regan (*puts her hand on Aaron's arm and stops walking*): Do you hear that?

Aaron (*turning around*): Kailey, is that you?

Kailey (*sitting at her desk in the back of the room, sniffling*): Yeah, it's me.

Aaron (*walking toward Kailey*): What's wrong?

Kailey (*quietly*): That test. I really needed to pass it.

Regan (*standing by the classroom door*): Kailey, you always do great in this class. I'm sure you did better than you think.

Aaron (*handing Kailey a tissue*): It was definitely a hard test. I'm sure if Professor Greenlee sees that some of his best students bombed it, he'll give us another chance or at least something to do for extra credit.

Kailey (*standing up with a slight smile and wiping her eyes with the tissue*): Let's keep our fingers crossed.

Which character was the most concerned about the chemistry test?

_____

How could you tell?

_____

Which character showed the most concern for his or her classmate?

_____

What indicated this concern?

_____

After reading the script, you probably recognized that Kailey was the most concerned about the test. The stage directions indicated that she didn't leave the classroom when everyone else did, she was sniffling, and she needed to wipe her eyes. Aaron seemed to show the most concern for her. The stage directions show that he went back into the room to talk with her and handed her a tissue. Without reading the stage directions, you still would have gotten the basic idea of what was happening in the drama, but you would have missed out on some important information that let you know the extent of the characters' emotions. You also would not have been aware of how one of the characters showed compassion and was helpful toward another.

TIP

Stage directions can also help reveal a character's personality. Think about the kind of person Aaron is in the example. Words such as *compassionate*, *kindhearted*, and *caring* may come to mind. If they do, it is probably because of what you read in the stage directions.

one character, or it may include many characters that are each involved in the story to varying degrees.

Another word for the main character in a story is the **protagonist**. This is the character in the story who has some type of problem to solve. The protagonist is commonly the "good guy," though this is not always the case. Any character who prevents the protagonist from solving his or her problem is an **antagonist**.

Story Elements

When you read a story, whether it is prose or drama, you can expect that something is going to happen to someone. Without at least this much, there would not be a story to tell. Just like a sentence needs a subject and a verb, a story needs characters and an event. The pieces that make up a story are the **story elements**. They include the following:

- characters
- setting
- plot
- resolution

Think of the story elements as the *who*, *where*, *when*, *what*, *why*, and *how* of the story. These work together to create a complete story that is interesting to readers, creates a clear understanding in the readers' minds, and answers all the readers' questions.

Characters

As you already know, the **characters** are the people, animals, or things that are involved in a story. These characters can be real or imaginary. Often, interesting characters are what get readers hooked on a story.

The **main character** or characters are those that the story is mostly about. A story may have as few as

Think about the example of *Goldilocks and the Three Bears* mentioned earlier. In this story, Goldilocks is the main character because the story is mostly about her adventures. Papa Bear, Mama Bear, and Baby Bear are the other characters in this story.

In *The Three Little Pigs*, each of the pigs and the wolf play an equally important role in the story. No one is featured more than the others, and the story is not mostly about any one of them. So, the three pigs and the wolf are all main characters.

In *Little Red Riding Hood*, Little Red and the wolf are the main characters because the story focuses on the events that happen to them. Little Red's mom, grandmother, and the woodcutter are all in the story, but not to the same extent as the main characters. In other words, during a play, they would not spend as much time on the stage as the main characters.

As discussed earlier, the characters in a drama are often introduced in the cast list at the beginning of the script. Readers get to know each of the characters through the dialogue and stage directions.

Throughout a story, readers get to know and understand the characters in many ways. **Characterization** refers to the way the characters' personalities, attitudes, appearances, and behaviors are revealed to the readers.

There are two types of characterization. **Direct characterization** is when a writer tells readers about a character's personality. He or she describes the character's personality, interests, actions, thoughts, feelings, speech, or appearance.

> *The shy little boy would not say a word in the large crowd.*

The writer directly tells readers that the boy is shy.

Indirect characterization shows readers a character's personality rather than telling them about it. Writers use indirect characterization to give readers insight about the characters in several ways. Indirect characterization often includes one or more of the following elements:

- **Actions and behavior.** What does the character do? How does he or she behave? What types of situations does he or she enjoy or avoid?
- **Speech.** What does the character say? How does he or she speak? What attitudes or beliefs are revealed by the character's speech?
- **Interactions with other characters.** How do other characters react to this character? What do they say about him or her?
- **Looks.** What does the character look like? How does he or she dress?

> *The little boy hid silently behind his mother's skirt and would not make eye contact with anyone.*

This sentence shows the character's personality rather than stating it directly. Readers can tell that the boy is shy through his actions and behavior.

A character's personality may change throughout the story or play, depending on the situation he or she is facing. For example, a businesswoman might be confident and strong at work, but could become timid and shy when giving a speech to a group of parents at her children's school.

As you read the following script, think about what the characters' words, thoughts, and actions reveal about their personalities.

Rebecca: *Sir, may I get you another slice of pie or more coffee?*

Mr. Daniels: *No, I ain't hungry no more. I've got to get goin' to make it to the market before they close. Can you tell me how much I gotta pay?*

Rebecca: *Absolutely. Your total today is $7.45. Would you like me to take that up to the register for you?*

Mr. Daniels (*showing Rebecca his money*): *I'll take it up to there. Is this how much money I need?*

Rebecca: *Well, sir, it looks like you need another quarter.*

Mr. Daniels: *Thank you. You've been a big help.*

Who are the characters in this script?

_____

What type of characterization does the writer use?

_____

What does this characterization reveal about the two characters?

_____

_____

In this script, the writer uses indirect characterization to share Rebecca and Mr. Daniels's personalities. You may have recognized that Rebecca is a waitress who is polite and helpful. This can be seen by the fact that she calls Mr. Daniels *sir* and offers to help him. You probably also recognized from the way he spoke and the fact that he needed help counting the money that Mr. Daniels, the customer, is not a highly educated man.

Setting

The **setting** refers to the time, place, and atmosphere where the story happens. This is the *when* and *where* of the story. It involves the following aspects:

- *Time*—time of day or night, season of the year, or historical period. Examples include Saturday afternoon, the middle of winter, and the 21st century.
- *Place*—location or geographical area, such as the school gymnasium, the midwestern United States, or New York City.
- *Atmosphere*—emotions that are related to the environment. For example, a haunted house can create fearful or nervous feelings, while a birthday party can create feelings of happiness or excitement.

The setting can help create the mood, give a picture of the action, and provide readers with insight into how the characters live. For example, if you know that a story takes place in Iceland, you will have certain ideas about the characters' lives and be able to form a mental picture of what type of clothing, activities, and towns the story will involve. If you know that a story is set during the colonial period, you will know that the characters had horses and buggies rather than cars, lived in small towns rather than big cities, and did not have electronics or other modern conveniences.

Consider the following example:

Ethan: *What are you doing after school today?*

Joey: *I've got to get my chores done as soon as I get home.*

Ethan: *Me, too. Do you want to get together and go swimming after that?*

Joey: *I'm sure my parents will let me, as long as my work is done and I'm home before dark.*

What picture do you have in your mind about the boys' afternoon? Think about what chores they probably have to do. Think about where they might be planning to go swimming. If you imagined that the setting is a modern-day city, you might have figured the boys needed to take out the recycling, mow the lawn, or load the dishwasher before they meet at the pool.

Now, suppose the story indicated that the setting was a farm town during the early 1800s. Chores likely included gathering eggs from the chickens, milking the cows, collecting water from the well, or helping plow the fields. After their work was done, the boys would swim in the river or lake. It is also understandable that the boys would need to be home before dark because there were no streetlights.

TIP

Remember that in a drama, a new scene begins each time the setting changes.

Setting can be directly stated by the author or left for readers to infer through the events and details in the text. In a drama, stage directions often indicate the setting.

That evening, we went for a long walk on the beach. There is not a more relaxing place on earth.

The author directly states the time, place, and atmosphere of the action in this sentence. The story takes place on the beach in the evening, and the atmosphere is relaxing.

After dinner, we went for a stroll and watched the sunset. There is nothing more soothing than feeling the sand between your toes and hearing the waves crashing on the shore.

Here, the writer implies the setting. *After dinner* and *sunset* indicate that the action took place in the evening. *Sand between your toes and waves crashing on the shore* indicate that the location of the story is at the beach. *Stroll* and *soothing* indicate a relaxed feeling.

Now you try it. As you read, keep in mind what you've reviewed about setting.

Reace (slamming her book closed): How are we ever going to get all this math finished by Friday?

Tyra (whispering): SHH! You can't be so loud in here! Ms. Rodriguez takes her job as assistant librarian very seriously and will have an absolute fit it we don't keep it down.

Reace: Tell me about it. She saw my MP3 player one day and made me put it in my backpack. It wasn't even on at the time.

Tyra (closing her books and putting them in her backpack): Well, we'd better hurry if we want to make it to homeroom on time this morning. We'll deal with math homework again after school. Let's go.

What is the setting of the drama?

- Time _____
- Place _____
- Atmosphere _____

This is an example of a writer implying the setting without directly stating it. The girls are in a hurry to get to homeroom, indicating that the action is taking place in school in the morning before classes begin. Because school is the setting, we also know that it is during the school year, on a weekday. The mention of an MP3 player lets readers know that the story occurs during modern times. Because the girls have to be quiet so as not to upset the assistant librarian, readers can figure out that the location of the action is in the library, which indicates a quiet, academic atmosphere.

Who are the characters in this short drama? If you said Reace and Tyra, you're absolutely correct! Ms. Rodriguez was mentioned but was not actually in the story, so she is not one of the characters.

Plot

The sequence of events that takes place from the beginning to the end of a story or play is the **plot**. In very simple terms, the plot is what happens in the story.

The plot will contain some sort of **conflict**, or problem, that the character or characters face. Usually, this conflict is introduced in the early parts of the story or play. Most of the events of the story revolve around this conflict and the actions that take place as the characters deal with and try to solve the problem.

The events that lead up to the climax of the story make up the **rising action**. The **climax** is the most dramatic moment, or the high point of the story. It creates the most interest and suspense and is generally the most exciting part of the story, where the characters are under the most stress. At this point in the story, something will happen to reveal how the conflict will be solved.

Jerome had only three weeks left to raise the money he needed to go on the ski trip, and he had no idea how to come up with such a large chunk of change. His parents promised to pay half, if he could earn the other half of the cost. It would be an expensive trip but undoubtedly worth the sacrifice. Jerome made up fliers for his lawn service and distributed them around the neighborhood, but no one replied. Who really needed a lawn service in the middle of the winter anyway? He went to the mall and responded to every "Help Wanted" sign. But, unfortunately, every store manager said the same thing: "Come back after your sixteenth birthday." Jerome was desperate. He was nearly out of ideas and about to pack his skis back in the attic. Then, the phone rang.

"Jerome," the voice said, "I need a huge favor."

What is the conflict in the story?
a. Jerome's phone rang.
b. Jerome had his own lawn service.
c. Jerome needed to earn money for the ski trip.
d. Jerome was too young to be able to earn any money.
e. Jerome's parents needed to pay for half of the ski trip.

Jerome's problem was that he needed to earn money to go on the ski trip (choice c). The rest of the story revolves around how Jerome tried to solve this problem.

Which events in the story comprise the rising action?

_____

_____

The events that lead up to the climax make up the rising action. These include Jerome making up and distributing lawn service fliers and applying for jobs at the mall.

What event is the climax of the story?

_____

Did you recognize the phone call as being the high point of the story? This is where Jerome is under the most stress, and suspense and excitement are building. The phone call suggests that things are about to change for Jerome.

Resolution

The point of the story where the conflict ends or the problem is solved is the **resolution**. This is usually toward the very end of the story.

The resolution is followed by the **denouement**, which is where life returns to normal for the characters, and they no longer have to deal with the conflict.

Let's find out how Jerome's problem is resolved.

Then, the phone rang.

"Jerome," the voice said, "I need a huge favor."

It was Jerome's neighbor, Dr. Cole, a veterinarian. "One of my employees is leaving town unexpectedly, leaving me shorthanded in the office. I really need someone who can stop by twice a day to help feed and water the animals in the kennel, take the dogs for a walk, and help groom the dogs and cats. It would only be for about three weeks, but I could really use your help. I'll pay you what I usually pay my employee."

Jerome was thrilled. "I'd be glad to do it, Dr. Cole! I am still trying to get together the money for that ski trip, so this opportunity couldn't have come at a better time," Jerome explained excitedly.

"It sounds like this will work out perfectly for both of us," the doctor replied. "I'll tell you what—you stop by my office before and after school every day for the next three weeks, and I'll be sure you have enough money for your trip, plus a little extra for spending money. You can start tomorrow morning at 6 a.m. sharp."

Jerome breathed a huge sigh of relief. Smiling, he finished his homework and got his clothes ready for the next day. He wanted to be sure he was on time for his first day of work.

Now, read the following question. Circle the best answer.

What is the resolution?
a. Jerome's phone rings.
b. Dr. Cole's employee goes out of town.
c. Jerome explains that he needs money.
d. Dr. Cole hires Jerome to help with the animals.
e. Jerome gets ready for his first day of work.

The resolution is the solution to the conflict. Remember, the conflict was that Jerome needed to earn money. Which of the answer choices solves this problem? Dr. Cole hires Jerome (choice **d**).

Which of the answer choices is the denouement?
a. Jerome's phone rings.
b. Dr. Cole's employee goes out of town.
c. Jerome explains that he needs money.
d. Dr. Cole hires Jerome to help with the animals.
e. Jerome gets ready for his first day of work.

Here are the same answer choices, but this question asks about a different point in the plot. After the problem is solved, Jerome gets ready for his first day of work by finishing his homework and getting his clothes ready for the next day. This shows his life getting back to normal, without the worry of the conflict. Choice **e** is the denouement.

Making Predictions

Whether you realize it or not, you make predictions every day. You consider a situation and make an educated guess about what will probably happen next. You go to soccer practice because you can guess that practicing will make you a better player. You put on your coat and mittens before going out in the snow because you know that you'll probably get cold if you leave home without them.

Considering information and making an educated guess about what is likely to happen next is called **making predictions**, and making predictions about what you are reading can help you better understand the text.

As you read, think about what has happened so far, predict what you think will probably happen next, then read on to check your predictions. Change your predictions and make new ones as you continue reading.

To make predictions, consider the following:

- passage or chapter titles
- headings
- key words
- charts and graphs
- maps and diagrams
- illustrations and captions
- what you already know
- what you have already read

Read the following text and think about what might happen next.

Morgan looked out the window. Thick gray clouds covered the sky. The trees in her backyard were bent over in the gusting winds, and leaves whipped quickly past the window. Suddenly, there was a bright flash of lightning, and a deafening crack of thunder shook the house.

Think about what you read, and think about what you already know. Think about when you may have experienced a day that is similar to what Morgan is seeing. Think about what usually happens on such days. Now make a prediction. What do you predict will happen next? It is likely that Morgan is about to experience some stormy weather.

You may have predicted that the power will go out at Morgan's house. You also might have predicted that she will turn on the TV or a battery-powered radio to hear the weather report. Or, you may have predicted that she ran outside to make sure the car windows were closed. Any of these are things that someone might do in such weather.

As you read, try to make connections between what you already know and clues that the author gives in the text, then think about what might happen next. Making predictions and thinking about what you are reading can help you better understand the material.

> To make predictions, ask yourself questions such as:
>
> - What will probably happen next?
> - What problem might the character face?
> - How will this problem be solved?
> - What will the passage teach me about the topic?

Drawing Conclusions

Suppose you walk into a pizza restaurant on a Friday night. The room is full of high school-aged guys wearing matching football jerseys. They are all laughing, cheering, and appear to be in generally great moods. A few men wearing shirts with matching logos are walking around, hugging the guys, patting them on the back, and congratulating them. Using the information you have collected, you can probably figure out that this is a high school football team celebrating tonight's victory with the coaches.

Drawing conclusions means using information to make a sensible guess about what is happening. The conclusion should be based on facts and details from the reading material. When you read, you must think about the information in the text as well as what you already know.

> I walked into the dark room and waited by the entrance for my eyes to adjust. The smell of popcorn filled the air as I squinted and blinked my eyes, looking for a row that had three empty seats together. Just then, images began to fill the huge screen in front of me. Very quickly, I turned off my cell phone. Then, I quietly hurried to sit down.

What conclusion can be drawn regarding where the speaker is? The author gave several helpful hints. Now, you must read between the lines a bit and add the information from the paragraph to what you already know:

- The room is dark.
- The smell of popcorn fills the air.
- There are rows of seats.
- A huge screen is at the front.
- The speaker felt it was important to be quiet.

You probably concluded that the speaker is in a movie theater. Being able to draw conclusions is one way that readers are able to better understand a text. Keep in mind that conclusions are not random guesses about what is happening in a story; conclusions are based on facts, details, and information in the text as well as your own prior knowledge.

Read the following script, think about what hints the author gives, consider what you already know, and then draw conclusions to determine what is happening in the passage.

Debbie (*shaking her head and looking around the room*): Will all these boxes ever get put away?

Mark: *It's only been a couple of days. Look how much we've done already. The family room, kitchen, and den are completely finished. All we really have left are the bedrooms.*

Olivia (*running into the room carrying a rag doll*): Look! I found Molly! She got mixed up in a box with my nightgowns and pajamas. Now all that's missing is Mr. Flopsy.

Debbie (*putting her arm around Olivia*): I'm sure you'll find your stuffed rabbit in no time. He's here somewhere.

Mark: *That's right. We'll unpack all our favorite things and be settled before you know it.*

Based on the information in the passage and what you already know, what conclusions can be drawn?

_____

You already know that people unpack boxes when they move. The family room, kitchen, den, and bedrooms are rooms in a house, and people unpack their favorite things and get settled in a new home. You can therefore draw the conclusion that the family is moving into a new home.

You also know that a rag doll and stuffed rabbit are things that usually belong to children. Because the text said that Olivia was excited about finding these items, you can conclude that Olivia is a child.

Quiz

Now that you've had a chance to review some of the skills needed to comprehend drama, give the questions that follow a try.

Directions: Read each script and choose the *one best answer* to each question.

Questions 1 through 6 refer to the following passage.

What Can Megan Do?
Act I, Scene I

Kailyn and Mom

Kailyn (sitting at the kitchen table with Mom, looking over a notebook, pencil in hand): As soon as everyone gets here on Friday night, let's order pizzas. Then we can set up the karaoke machine and sing for awhile.

Mom: That sounds like fun! Where are you planning to spread out the sleeping bags?

Kailyn: I was thinking we'd put them in the family room, so we can crawl into them to watch movies later.

Mom: You know Megan is going to want to be involved in some of the festivities, too, don't you?

Kailyn (disappointed, drops her pencils on the table and sighs): But, Mom, she is four years younger than me. Why does she have to be in the middle of everything?

Mom: This is her house, too, honey. I understand that you don't want her with you all night long, but you can't exclude her completely. You need to come up with a way to let her be involved without interfering.

Act I, Scene 2

Kailyn and Natalia

Kailyn (walking home from school the next day): So, my mom says Megan has to be a part of things on Friday night. That is so unfair, don't you think?

Natalia: Well, my mom would probably do the same thing.

Kailyn: I don't want her dragging her little pink ballerina sleeping bag into the room and planning to stay up with us all night. If she has to be involved, it needs to be earlier than bedtime.

Natalia: You've got to think of something for her to do that wouldn't be invading the party, but would still let her feel like she was included.

Act I, Scene 3

Kailyn and Megan

Kailyn (sitting on her bed, looking over her list of party plans, thinking aloud to herself): There's got to be something she would like to do without being in the way, but what?

(Kailyn hears Megan singing from the next room.)

Kailyn (excitedly): I've got it!

(Kailyn runs to Megan's room.)

Kailyn: We're going to set up the karaoke machine on Friday night. How would you like to sing with us?

Megan (jumping up and down excitedly): That would be awesome! I know just what to sing! Thank you!

Kailyn (smiling at Megan): You'll do a great job. You really do have a very pretty voice. It will be fun.

(Kailyn hugs Megan, then walks back to her room, smiling.)

1. Which characters are in Scene 2?
   a. Kailyn and Mom
   b. Kailyn and Megan
   c. Kailyn and Natalia
   d. Kailyn, Mom, and Megan
   e. Kailyn, Natalia, Mom, and Megan

2. Where does the first scene take place?
   a. the kitchen
   b. family room
   c. walking home
   d. Kailyn's room
   e. Megan's room

3. Who is Megan?
   a. Kailyn's sister
   b. Kailyn's friend
   c. Natalia's sister
   d. Kailyn and Natalia's friend
   e. Mom and Kailyn's neighbor

4. What is the main reason Kailyn's friends are coming over on Friday night?
   a. pizza party
   b. slumber party
   c. birthday party
   d. karaoke contest
   e. movie screening

5. What is the conflict in the story?
   a. Megan has to be involved in the party.
   b. Kailyn is having a party on Friday night.
   c. Everyone will be bringing sleeping bags.
   d. Natalia says her mom would agree with Kailyn's.
   e. The friends are going to use the karaoke machine.

6. What is the resolution?
   a. Megan jumps up and down excitedly.
   b. Kailyn returns to her bedroom, smiling.
   c. Kailyn invites Megan to sing karaoke with her friends.
   d. Mom gives Kailyn news that she does not want to hear.
   e. Megan brings her sleeping bag to the family room with the others.

Questions 7 through 10 refer to the following passage.

Who Will Emilio Choose?

Act I, Scene 1

Honors Club meeting in Mr. O'Hare's classroom

Mr. O'Hare, Emilio, Honors Club members

Mr. O'Hare (speaking to a group of students): Well, it looks like we have a three-way tie. Ling, Emma, and Charlie each got the same number of votes for vice president. Emilio, since you're president of the honors club, it's up to you to choose the best candidate for the job.

Emilio (surprised): Seriously? How can I do that? These are all my friends. I couldn't choose between them.

Mr. O'Hare (speaking gently): I know this is a huge decision, and it won't be an easy one, but I'm confident that you'll know who would be the best person for the job. You can take until Friday to decide.

Act I, Scene 2

School hallway

Emilio, Ling, and Charlie

Ling (walking up to Emilio at his locker): Hey, Emilio. I baked brownies for you last night. They're double dark chocolate, your favorite!

Emilio (opening the box and smelling the brownies): Wow, thanks!

Ling: Also, if you need any help mowing lawns after school, just let me know. Or, if want me to check out the books you need for your research paper, I can do that for you. Whatever you need.

(Ling walks away.)

Emilio (suspiciously): Um, thanks.

Charlie (walking up to Emilio): Hey, Mr. President, what's up?

Emilio: Not much, man.

Charlie (pulling his report card out of his backpack): Just wanted you to take a look at this. Check it out. All A's, as always. Don't you think the V.P. of the honors club should make straight A's?

Emilio: Well, doesn't everyone in the club pretty much have all A's?

Charlie (stepping closer to Emilio and speaking quietly): Well, I heard that Ling might end up with a B in chemistry. She had a stomach flu and missed the review day before a big test. Better than that, Emma got a D on our last algebra quiz. She'd been visiting her grandma in the hospital and didn't study.

Emilio: Didn't the teacher say she could retake the quiz because of the circumstances?

Charlie: Well, yeah. But, dude, she got a D!

Act I, Scene 3

Picnic tables in the schoolyard

Emilio and Emma

Emma: Hey, Emilio! Got a minute? I know you've got to make a tough decision and wanted to tell you that I won't have any hard feelings if you choose Charlie or Ling. They both deserve to be vice president. I don't envy you having to do this, but you'll make the right decision.

Emilio (smiling gently and nodding his head): You know what? I just did.

7. Which word best describes Charlie?
   a. devious
   b. friendly
   c. irritated
   d. sincere
   e. suspicious

8. Based on the information in the text, what did Emilio most likely do?
   a. He chose Ling to be the vice president.
   b. He chose Emma to be the vice president.
   c. He chose Charlie to be the vice president.
   d. He asked Mr. O'Hare to select someone for the position.
   e. He asked Mr. O'Hare to select someone by a random drawing.

9. Which is a rising action in the script?
   a. An election is held to choose the vice president of the Honors Club.
   b. Mr. O'Hare announces the results of the election for vice president.
   c. Ling bakes Emilio's favorite brownies and offers to help him.
   d. Emilio makes a decision about who should have the job.
   e. The new vice president of the Honors Club begins work.

10. What will most likely happen next?
   a. Emma will accept her nomination as vice president.
   b. Mr. O'Hare will choose a vice president.
   c. Charlie and Ling will quit the honors club.
   d. Emilio will step down as president of the honors club.
   e. Emilio will petition to get Charlie, Ling, and Emma to serve as co-vice presidents.

Answers

1. c. Kailyn and Natalia are the characters in this scene. Theirs are the only names in the cast list at the beginning of the scene, and theirs are the only names listed before the dialogue. Megan and Mom were both mentioned in this scene, but they did not appear in it.

2. a. The stage directions indicate that the first scene takes place with Kailyn sitting at the kitchen table. The family room is mentioned during that scene, but that is not the setting. Scene 2 takes place as the girls walk home from school, and scene 3 takes place in Kailyn and Megan's bedrooms.

3. a. The writer does not directly state who Megan is but does give hints. We know that she lives in the same house with Kailyn, and Mom says she has to be involved in what goes on there. Based on what we already know about families, we can conclude that Megan must be Kailyn's sister.

4. b. The writer never states that Kailyn is having a slumber party, but there are plenty of clues that lead readers to that conclusion. The biggest clue is that the friends will be setting up sleeping bags. Based on what we already know, guests bring sleeping bags to slumber parties. There is no indication that the party is for anyone's birthday. They will be ordering pizza, but it is not a pizza party. They are also planning to use the karaoke machine, but there is nothing indicating that there will be a contest. Kailyn is planning to show movies, but the party is not a movie screening.

5. a. The conflict is the problem that the characters must face throughout the story. Answer choices **b**, **c**, **d**, and **e** are all events that occurred, but they are not problems that must be solved. Kailyn spends the majority of the story trying to find a way for Megan to be involved in the party.

6. c. The resolution occurs toward the very end of a story and solves a problem. Kailyn inviting Megan to sing karaoke solves the problem in the story. Answer choice **d** occurs at the beginning of the story. Answer choices **a** and **b** occur after the resolution and are part of the denouement. Kailyn is afraid that answer choice **e** will happen, but it does not.

7. a. The writer used indirect characterization to reveal Charlie's personality. He told Emilio negative things about the other candidates in order to make himself appear to be the best person for the position. He stepped closer to Emilio and spoke quietly, showing that he was trying to be sneaky, or *devious*.

8. b. You probably recognized from his comments that Emilio was suspicious of Ling's and Charlie's motives. He seemed to recognize that Ling was up to something. He also did not seem to appreciate Charlie's comments about the other candidates. When Emma was straightforward, Emilio said he had just made his decision. It would be logical to conclude that he chose Emma. Nothing indicated that he would ask Mr. O'Hare to decide or that he would hold a drawing to choose the vice president.

9. c. The rising actions are the events that happen as the characters work toward solving the conflict. The election is held and the results are announced before the problem is introduced. Emilio's decision resolves the conflict, and the new vice president begins his or her term after the story ends. Ling baking brownies and offering to help Emilio are some of the events that lead up to the resolution of the conflict.

10. a. Having concluded that Emilio selected Emma to be his vice president, we can predict that she will accept the nomination—after all, she ran for the position. There is no indication that Mr. O'Hare will select a vice president for Emilio—he wants Emilio to make tough decisions. Although Charlie and Ling may be upset about not being chosen, we have no reason to believe that they will quit, nor is there any indication that Emilio will step down. Based on the suspicious characterizations of Charlie and Ling, Emilio would probably not want them serving as co-vice presidents alongside Emma.

In this chapter, you learned several strategies to help you better comprehend reading materials, especially dramatic works:

1. A drama is a written work that is intended to be acted out on a stage. The majority of the writing consists of dialogue between characters.
2. The cast list, acts, scenes, dialogue, and stage directions are all parts of a script.
3. The pieces that make up a story written as drama or prose are known as story elements and include characters, settings, plot, and resolution.
4. The people, animals, and creatures involved in a story are the characters. A writer uses characterization to let readers know what the characters are like. Their speech, actions, behavior, and relationships with others give insight about a character to the readers.
5. Plot is the sequence of events that occur from the beginning of the story to the end. It includes a conflict, or problem, that the characters must resolve.
6. The resolution is how the conflict in a story is resolved.
7. Readers draw conclusions by combining information from the text with their own prior knowledge to make reasonable guesses about what is happening in the text.
8. Making predictions can help readers monitor their own understanding of the text. This involves considering the information in the passage as well as what you already know and making an educated guess about what will most likely happen next.

CHAPTER

6 ▶ NONFICTION

CHAPTER SUMMARY

This chapter helps you with the nonfiction passages that make up a quarter of the GED® Language Arts, Reading test. It teaches you to identify main ideas and supporting details, summarize passages, distinguish fact from opinion, recognize organizational structure, and make inferences.

So far, we've reviewed several types of fiction literature. In this chapter, we review strategies for better understanding nonfiction text. **Nonfiction** is factual writing that discusses real-life people, places, events, and topics. Simply stated, nonfiction texts are true.

The following are examples of nonfiction texts:

- textbooks
- newspapers
- encyclopedias
- magazine articles
- reference materials
- speeches
- research papers

- training manuals
- legal documents
- employee handbooks
- biographies and autobiographies
- memoirs
- essays
- reviews of literature or the arts

On the GED Language Arts, Reading exam, you will read nonfiction as well as fiction texts. In fact, 25% of the material you will read will be nonfiction. There will be two nonfiction selections from two of the following three areas:

- nonfiction prose
- review of visual or performing arts
- workplace or community documents

The types of workplace and community documents that may appear on the test include business mission and goal statements, employee handbook materials, legal documents, communications such as letters or memos, and excerpts from various types of manuals. Like the fiction passages, each nonfiction passage will include between 200 and 400 words and be followed by a set of four to eight questions.

Several strategies can be helpful in fully comprehending nonfiction text. Understanding the main idea and supporting details, summarizing materials, distinguishing between fact and opinion, recognizing organizational structure, and making inferences are all ways to gain a deeper understanding of what you read. Keep in mind that although these strategies are often associated with nonfiction materials, they can be beneficial when reading other types of texts as well.

Main Idea and Supporting Details

Every passage you read, regardless of the type of material, has a main idea. The **main idea**, sometimes called the *big idea*, is the central message of the text. To determine the main idea, first identify the topic of the text. Then, think about the major point that the writer is trying to tell readers about the topic. For example, if the topic of a passage is loggerhead sea turtles, the main idea could be as follows:

Loggerhead sea turtles return to the beach where they were born to lay eggs.

This would be the most important idea that the writer wants you to take away from the passage. The rest of the passage would contain information to help explain the main idea. Examples, information, facts, and details that help to explain and describe the main idea are the **supporting details**. These help to strengthen readers' understanding of the main idea.

In the passage about sea turtles, supporting details could include the following sentences:

The turtles crawl onto the beach at night.

They dig a hole in the sand and lay their eggs in the hole.

After covering the nest with sand, the turtles return to the ocean.

Each of these supporting details gives information about the main idea.

There are four basic types of supporting details that writers include to give readers a deeper understanding of the central message of the text. Here are the types of supporting details:

- examples
- reasons
- facts
- descriptions

Being able to identify the main idea and supporting details is helpful in organizing the information in a passage. Readers are able to recognize the central message of the text and identify examples, reasons, facts, and descriptions to clarify and explain the message.

While the topic of a passage may be as short as a single word, the main idea of a passage is always a complete sentence.

Read the following paragraph. Look for the main idea and supporting details as you read.

Before becoming the sixteenth president of the United States, Abraham Lincoln showed a pattern of behavior that caused him to earn the nickname "Honest Abe." Early in his career, he worked in the grocery business. When his partner passed away, leaving behind a mountain of debt, Lincoln not only paid off his own part of the money, but also his late partner's share because this was the honest thing to do. Later, he worked as a lawyer. During that time in history, members of the legal profession were often recognized as being dishonest. However, Lincoln earned the reputation among his colleagues as being a man who never told a lie. He even gave a lecture during which he encouraged the audience to make honesty a priority in their occupations.

What is the main idea of the passage?

_____

You probably recognized that the first sentence tells the main idea of the passage. You may have stated that the main idea is:

Abraham Lincoln earned the nickname "Honest Abe."

Abraham Lincoln showed a pattern of honesty throughout his life.

People called Lincoln "Honest Abe" because of the priority he placed on honesty.

Any of these would be correct. The main idea is the most important piece of information, about which the rest of the paragraph is written. Each of these choices captures that information.

Which of the following is a supporting detail from the passage?
   a. Abraham Lincoln was the sixteenth president of the United States.
   b. Lincoln's behavior caused him to be known as "Honest Abe."
   c. Early in his career, Lincoln worked in the grocery business.
   d. Members of the legal profession were known for being dishonest.
   e. Lincoln's colleagues recognized him as a man who never told a lie.

Did you recognize that answer choice **e** supports the main idea of the passage? This statement is an example of the honesty that caused people to call Lincoln "Honest Abe." Choice **b** restates the main idea. Choices **a**, **c**, and **d** all contain relevant or interesting information, but they do not directly support the main idea, so they are considered minor details rather than supporting details.

What other supporting details are contained in the passage?

_____

_____

Supporting details from the passage include *Lincoln paid off his late partner's debt as well as his own* and *he gave a lecture encouraging the audience to be honest.* These statements support the main idea by giving some reasons why he became known for his honesty.

Some reading passages include more than a single paragraph. Every paragraph will have its own main idea. The main idea is stated in the topic sentence. The **topic sentence** basically sums up what the entire paragraph tries to explain.

Look back at the paragraph about Lincoln. Can you identify the topic sentence? It is the sentence that tells the basic message of the paragraph.

Before becoming the sixteenth president of the United States, Abraham Lincoln showed a pattern of behavior that caused him to earn the nickname "Honest Abe."

This is the first sentence of the paragraph, and it is the topic sentence. Notice that it also contains the main idea. The topic sentence can be anywhere in the paragraph; however, it is generally either the first or last sentence. Being able to locate the topic sentence can be helpful in determining the main idea.

TIP

Sometimes, the main idea is suggested but not directly stated. Remember to ask yourself what the topic is and what the most important thought is about the topic. This will help you determine the main idea of the text.

Summarizing

Have you ever given a book report or written a research paper? In either case, you read information from a text, then restated the most important ideas in your own words. This is called **summarizing**.

Being able to summarize information is one way to show how well you understood what you read because it requires you to focus on the main points and explain them. Think back to a research paper you have written. Chances are, you read a number of articles or books about your topic; however, your paper

was probably only a few pages long. That's because you only included key pieces of information in your summary. You chose the main idea and the most important supporting details and restated these in the report.

Think back about the paragraph we read about "Honest Abe." What information in the text was the most important? How could you restate that in your own words?

Abraham Lincoln was known as "Honest Abe" for many reasons. He showed honesty in his early work life, set an example of honesty as a lawyer working among many dishonest colleagues, and encouraged others to practice honesty as well.

This summary has two sentences in it. The original paragraph about Lincoln was considerably longer. Because a summary focuses only on the most important information, it is generally much shorter than the original text. In fact, you might summarize an entire book in only a few sentences or paragraphs.

Read the following paragraph.

In the midst of New York Harbor stands a 305-foot tall, 225-ton symbol of freedom and democracy: the Statue of Liberty. "Lady Liberty," as she is affectionately known, was a gift of friendship from France and was dedicated on October 28, 1886. Officially named "The Statue of Liberty Enlightening the World," this highly recognizable structure contains much symbolism. For example, the torch itself is a symbol of enlightenment. The tablet of law held in her left hand contains Roman numerals representing the date of our country's independence, July 4, 1776. Finally, the crown on the head of the statue has seven rays, one for each of the seven continents.

The statue is covered in copper, about the thickness of two pennies. Natural weathering has caused the copper to turn a light green color.

When the statue was restored for its 100th birthday, the torch was replaced, and the new torch was covered with a thin layer of 24 karat gold. During the day, the sun's reflection lights the torch; at night, it is lighted by 16 floodlights.

To summarize the passage,

- determine the most important idea.
- decide what information can be left out.
- restate the information using your own words.

Now, let's summarize the passage.

What is the main idea of the entire passage?

_____

_____

What are two important supporting details?

_____

_____

Write a summary of the passage in your own words.

_____

_____

_____

You probably recognized that the main idea is one of the following:

The Statue of Liberty is an important symbol.

The Statue of Liberty is a huge monument that represents many things.

Remember, there is not a single correct way to state the main idea. The important thing is that you recognize which information is the most important.

Next, figure out which supporting details are key. The size of the Statue of Liberty is definitely interesting. It could even be the central idea of another passage. However, in this example, these facts are not some of the supporting details that must find their way into a summary. The same is true about the date the statue was dedicated and the fact that the copper has turned green over the past century and a half. These are all ideas that could be left out when you summarize the passage.

The most important supporting details would be those that address the symbolism associated with the statue. Information about the significance of the torch, the tablet, and the crown should be included in a thorough summary.

TIP

Don't forget! A summary must use your own words, not the words of the author. Restate the ideas that you read and make sure you are not copying what is written in the text.

Just like the main idea, there is more than one correct way to summarize a passage. Yours may be similar to the following summary:

The Statue of Liberty was a gift from France that symbolizes a number of ideas that are important to our country. The torch represents enlightenment, the tablet recognizes the date of our country's freedom, and the crown acknowledges the seven continents in the world.

Remember learning that each paragraph has its own main idea? See if you can find the main idea in the second paragraph about "Lady Liberty." If you recognized the main idea as the fact that the Statue of Liberty is coated with a thin layer of copper, you're exactly right! Supporting details include information about the thickness of the copper and the fact that it has changed colors due to weathering.

TIP

Words such as *beautiful, best, worst, should, terrible,* and *wonderful* often indicate an opinion. Look for clues that help you determine that a statement shares the feelings or beliefs of the author.

Fact and Opinion

You probably learned the difference between fact and opinion when you were younger. A **fact** is a true statement that can be proven.

California is located on the west coast of the United States.

This is a fact. Look at any atlas, encyclopedia, or geography book, and you can verify, or prove, that this statement is true.

An **opinion** is a statement that reflects someone's personal views. Not everyone will agree with an opinion.

California's beaches are the most beautiful in the whole country.

Many people would probably agree with this statement. However, this is the writer's personal view. If you were to talk with people sitting on the beaches in Hawaii, North Carolina, or Florida, you'd most likely find at least a few who disagree.

Writers often use a combination of facts and opinions to share their ideas. Being able to distinguish between these statements can help you gain a complete understanding of the passage. Strong readers are able to interpret the information in a passage and form their own opinions.

Four inches of snow fell overnight.

Can this be proven? Absolutely. A ruler or a weather report can be used to check how much snow fell. Because this statement can be proven, it is a fact.

We have had too much snow this winter.

Can this be proven? We could prove that snow has fallen, but how much is too much? Not everyone would agree that there has been too much snow. In fact, some people might think there has not been enough. This statement tells how someone feels about the snow, so it is an opinion.

Facts and opinions are both useful. They not only help writers get their point across; they can be useful to readers as well.

Suppose you want to buy tickets to a play and are trying to decide which play to attend. You would need to know facts such as where each play is being performed, the times and dates of the shows, and the cost of the tickets. These facts are helpful in making up your mind. But, you'll probably want to find some opinions, too. You could read reviews or talk to friends to find out which theaters offer the best seats, which actors and actresses are the most entertaining, and whether a particular play is completely boring.

The author's purpose for writing a piece can impact whether the text includes mostly facts, mostly opinions, or a combination of both:

- If the author's purpose is *to inform*, the text is likely to contain mostly facts.
- If the author's purpose is *to entertain*, a combination of facts and opinions will be included.
- If the author's purpose is *to persuade*, you can definitely expect to find opinions. However, facts that support or promote the author's opinion may also be included.

TIP

As you read nonfiction passages, look for facts that give information about the topic. If opinions are included, be sure to recognize them for what they are—the personal feelings of the writer, not verifiable information.

As you read the following paragraph, determine which statements are facts and which are opinions. Ask yourself:

1. Can this statement be proven or verified?
2. Would everyone agree with this statement?

The drama club of Meadowbrook Middle School put on a stage presentation of The Elves and the Shoemaker *earlier this month. The students performed before a sold-out crowd for all three performances. The highlight of the evening was a dance by the elves during the second act. Even the principal was seen laughing until tears filled her eyes. It was the first live performance the students put on this year, although plans for a spring musical were announced at the end of the evening. It is sure to be a huge success!*

A woodwind ensemble from the school band provided music before the show as well as during the intermission. This impressive group of young musicians was enjoyed by all. The amazing talent present in the school was obvious in everyone involved, from the actors and actresses to the stagehands and technical crew. Ticket sales for the performances earned nearly $900 for the school's fine arts department.

Did you determine which statements from the review of the play were facts and which were opinions?

Facts from the passage:

- The drama club of Meadowbrook Middle School put on a stage presentation of *The Elves and the Shoemaker* earlier this month.
- The students performed before a sold-out crowd for all three performances.
- Even the principal was seen laughing until tears filled her eyes.
- It was the first live performance the students put on this year, although plans for a spring musical were announced at the end of the evening.
- A woodwind ensemble from the school band provided music before the show as well as during the intermission.
- Ticket sales for the performances earned nearly $900 for the school's fine arts department.

Each of these statements could be proven by checking the school calendar, looking at the program for the performances, or checking with the accountant for the fine arts department. Even the statement about the principal could be verified through a photograph or video. She might even admit it.

Opinions from the passage:

- The highlight of the evening was a dance by the elves during the second act.
- It is sure to be a huge success!
- This impressive group of young musicians was enjoyed by all.

- The amazing talent present in the school was obvious in everyone involved, from the actors and actresses to the stagehands and technical crew.

All these are opinions because there could be people who would not agree with the author. For example, some audience members might have thought the highlight of the evening was when the musicians played, not when the elves danced. Also, *amazing* and *impressive* are words that often indicate an opinion.

Organizational Structure

When you write, whether the text is a story, a letter, or a research paper, you probably spend time planning the order in which you will present your ideas. It would not make sense to randomly write down your thoughts without any pattern or logical order. Before writing, you probably organize similar ideas together or tell actions and events in the order in which they happened. Without using some sort of organization, not only would you have trouble getting your thoughts across accurately, but your readers would also become terribly confused.

Writers want their texts to make sense. The whole point of writing is to share information and ideas with an audience, and writers carefully consider how to best arrange this information so that readers are able to follow their thoughts and fully understand the passage. The **organizational structure** of a passage is the way a writer arranges his or her ideas.

Common types of organizational structures that writers may choose include *sequence, cause and effect, compare and contrast, problem and solution, classification*, and *description*.

Understanding how information is presented can help readers

- organize and understand the passage.
- anticipate what ideas might be presented next.
- think about what information to look for.
- make predictions.
- connect ideas from different parts of the text.

To recognize which organizational structure an author has used, think about what he or she wants readers to know. If an author wants to be sure readers understand the order in which events occurred, sequence is probably used. If he or she wants readers to know what led up to a particular event, a cause and effect structure is likely to be found. Recognizing and understanding each type of organizational structure can make a big difference in how well you comprehend the material.

Now, let's talk about each type of organizational structure in a little more detail.

Sequence

The **sequence** of events is the order in which the events are discussed in a passage. When readers are able to recognize that a text uses a sequential organizational structure, they know that details, ideas, and events will be presented in a specific order. Often, the sequence used is either time order or order of importance.

Time order means that ideas and events are presented chronologically, or in the order in which they actually happened. Often, words and phrases such as the following indicate time order:

- first	- before
- second	- after that
- next	- following
- then	- by the time
- last	- as soon as

Writers often use time order when the correct order is important. For example, history books are often written in time order by beginning with the earliest events and leading up to the most recent. Correct order would also be important when readers are expected to follow steps in a particular sequence, such as directions, how-to articles, and recipes.

Of all days for it to happen, my alarm clock didn't go off this morning. As soon as I opened my eyes and saw sunlight, I knew it would be a race to make it to the bus on time. The first thing I did was jump in the shower, wash my hair quickly, then jump right back out. Next was the dash to the closet. Shirt on, jeans zipped, shoes tied, and down the stairs. By the time I reached the kitchen, Mom had my peanut butter toast wrapped in a napkin and ready to go. I ran out the door, and before it even slammed behind me, the bus pulled up to the curb. Yes! I made it!

Did you know that newspaper articles are often organized in order of importance? The most important information is usually listed at the beginning of the article, followed by less important information. The reason for this is that some readers do not take the time to finish the entire article. This organizational structure ensures that those readers do not miss the most important ideas.

The transition words in the paragraph help readers know exactly when each action happened. On the lines below, list the events of the paragraph in the correct order.

_____

_____

_____

_____

You probably figured out that the events occurred in this order:

1. The alarm clock did not go off.
2. The speaker opened his or her eyes.
3. The speaker showered.
4. The speaker got dressed.
5. Mom wrapped up the toast in a napkin.
6. The speaker ran out the door.
7. The bus reached the curb.
8. The door slammed.

Another sequence writers may use to organize their writing is by **order of importance**. They might choose to tell the most important idea first, followed by ideas that decrease in importance. This is a good way to catch the readers' attention by beginning with the strongest point.

Conversely, writers may begin by telling the least important idea, then list ideas or events in increasing order of importance, telling the most important idea last. This leaves readers with the strongest point freshest in their minds.

The Tri-City Tigers won the district soccer championship on Friday night! The final score was 5–2 in what was a very exciting game. Jackson Greenwood scored three goals for the Tigers. Coach Abbott placed each team member in the game at some point. It was truly a victory for all!

The fact that the Tigers won the championship is the most important idea in the paragraph, so it is stated at the beginning. The final score is the second most important piece of information, so it is stated next. Jackson scoring two goals is next in importance, followed by the fact that all the players were involved in the win.

If the writer had chosen to tell the events in order of least to most importance, the paragraph could have been organized as shown here:

All members of the Tigers soccer team got a chance to play in Friday night's game, thanks to Coach Abbott. Jackson Greenwood scored three goals for his team. The final score of the exciting game was 5–2, giving the Tri-City Tigers the title of district champs!

Cause and Effect

As you know, a *cause* is something that makes something else happen. An *effect* is what happens as a result of the cause. For example, if you go to bed late, you'll be tired in the morning. Going to bed late is the cause; being tired in the morning is the effect.

At times, there is a cause and effect relationship between events in a passage. Authors may choose to use a **cause and effect** organizational structure, which focuses on such relationships, in the text. Recognizing a cause and effect structure lets readers know that they should be on the lookout for things that are the result of a given event. It also helps readers understand how events in the passage are related to one another.

> *Darnell studied every night for a week, so he got an A on his science exam.*

How are these events related? Did one thing happen as a result of the other? Yes. Studying every night *caused* Darnell to do well on the test. He got an A *because* he studied so much. So, studying every night is the cause; getting an A on the exam is the effect.

Often, writers will include clues—words that signal a cause and effect relationship. Examples of such words are listed here:

- because
- then
- as a result
- so
- due to
- therefore
- since
- when
- if

> *Ella fixed French toast for breakfast since it was her parents' anniversary.*

In this sentence, the clue word *since* indicates a cause and effect relationship. In the sentence about Darnell, the clue word *so* signaled the relationship.

Notice that either the cause or the effect can come first. In Darnell's example, the cause is first; in Ella's example, the effect is first. To determine which event is the cause and which is the effect, ask yourself which event is the result of the other.

Now it's your turn. Read the following paragraph. As you read, look for cause and effect relationships.

> *During the past quarter, our company had a record number of sales. As a result, we also saw a significant increase in profits. So, over the next few weeks, we will be able to hire additional employees in several departments to take on some of the workload. Current employees will also receive a bonus in their next paycheck as recognition for their contribution to our company's continued success.*

What signal words were included to offer clues about the cause and effect relationships?

_____

As a result and *so* were used to highlight two of the relationships. However, you probably noticed that more than two relationships existed. Signal words are not always included. Be sure to read carefully and think about how the events in a passage are related, whether signal words are included or not.

Did you recognize all the cause and effect relationships in this paragraph?

The *cause*:

- a record number of sales for the company

The *effects*:

- a significant increase in profits
- the hiring of additional employees
- a bonus for current employees

Notice that a single cause had more than one effect. The opposite may also be true; a single effect can be the result of several causes.

Compare and Contrast

When we *compare*, we tell how two or more things are alike. When we *contrast*, we tell how two or more things are different. Writers often use a **compare and contrast** organizational structure to explain ideas, events, people, or objects by describing the ways in which they are alike or different. When readers recognize a compare and contrast structure in a passage, they look for similarities and differences between the topics.

Signal words often alert readers that things are alike or different in some way.

Similarities	Differences
■ also	■ but
■ like	■ yet
■ both	■ only
■ alike	■ differ
■ similar	■ unlike
■ likewise	■ rather
■ the same as	■ although
■ at the same time	■ however
■ in the same ways	■ different
■ in the same manner	■ less than
	■ better than
	■ nevertheless
	■ on the contrary

By comparing and contrasting, writers are able to help readers gain a clear understanding of their ideas.

Chinchillas are small animals that are slightly larger and rounder than squirrels. Both animals are generally gray or brown in color. The chinchilla often has a bushy tail similar to that of a squirrel, although its ears are more round, like those of a mouse.

The comparisons and contrasts in this paragraph help describe chinchillas in a way that gives readers a clear picture of these animals.

What signal words did you notice in the paragraph?

_____

You probably recognized that *slightly larger and rounder than, both, similar to, although,* and *like*

pointed out similarities and differences between the various animals.

There are two types of compare and contrast organizational structures that writers often use. **Whole-to-whole comparisons** completely discuss the first idea, event, or item and then completely discuss the second. For example, if a writer were comparing and contrasting sports, he might completely explain baseball, then completely describe soccer.

Part-to-part comparisons discuss one particular aspect of each topic, then discuss another aspect, and so on. For example, a writer might discuss the number of players on baseball and soccer teams, then discuss how points are scored in each game, and then discuss the rules for each game.

Problem and Solution

If an author elects to use a **problem and solution** organizational structure, a problem is discussed and is then followed by one or more solutions to the problem. When readers recognize this structure, they know that as they read, they should look for possible ways to solve the problem.

Construction of the new auditorium at Forest Lakes Middle School is scheduled to begin in early April, which will interfere with the school's planned Spring Fling Carnival, because construction equipment will occupy a large portion of the area normally used for the event. The carnival committee believes it may be possible to reschedule the carnival for the middle of March, prior to groundbreaking on the construction project. If that is not possible, the committee may consider moving some of the activities indoors, reducing the need for some of the outside space. It has also been suggested that an alternative location, such as the nearby Little League fields, be used for the event.

What problem is the topic of the paragraph?

_____

The problem is that there may not be enough space for the school carnival after construction has begun on the new auditorium.

What solutions are suggested?

_____

_____

_____

Three possible solutions are suggested: change the date of the carnival, move some of the activities indoors, and change the location of the event. In a longer passage, the problem might be introduced in one paragraph, with each solution being discussed in separate paragraphs.

Classification

Sometimes, writers divide information about a topic into smaller sections that each focus on a group of related ideas or objects. This organizational structure is called **classification**, and writers use it to arrange ideas and information into categories. Each category contains ideas that are similar in some way.

Readers can recognize that classification has been used if the passage talks about different kinds of things, such as different kinds of animals, different types of transportation, or different kinds of sports. This structure lets readers know that ideas in each section will be somehow related.

TIP

Sometimes, section headers will be a clue that the organizational structure is classification. For example, a passage about animals might include section headers such as *mammals, reptiles, birds, amphibians,* and *fish.*

Dear Friends,

We are pleased that you are planning a trip to our resort! We are sure that you will find the vacation package that best suits your needs. Vacation packages are grouped into three categories. You may make your selection at any time prior to your arrival.

Room-only packages include your hotel room and access to the resort's three swimming pools. You may also enjoy the exercise equipment in the gym at no additional charge.

Bed-and-breakfast packages include your hotel room as well as access to the pools and gym. Breakfast in any of the resort restaurants is also included, or you may choose to order your morning meal from our room service menu.

All-inclusive packages include not only the offerings of the previous packages, but also lunch and dinner from any of the resort restaurants or room service. Each guest may enjoy three meals and two snacks each day, all included in the price of the package.

We look forward to your stay and would be happy to answer any questions. Feel free to contact us at any time for further assistance.

Sincerely,

Resort Manager

This passage uses a classification organizational structure. What is the topic of the letter?

_____

_____

What were the categories that the information was divided into?

_____

You probably recognized that the topic is the resort's vacation packages, and the categories the packages are divided into include *room-only*, *bed-and-breakfast*, and *all-inclusive* options.

Description

When an author chooses a **description** as the organizational pattern for a passage, he or she will introduce the topic, then discuss attributes and characteristics that describe it. When readers recognize this organizational pattern, they know to anticipate finding details, attributes, examples, and characteristics that will help explain the topic.

> *For more than 200 years, the White House has been home to the presidents of the United States and is undoubtedly the most recognizable residence in the country. A view of the front reveals a two-story structure with rows of rectangular windows, columns in the center of the building, and our nation's flag flying over the roof. Indoors, the home boasts six levels, including 132 rooms, 35 restrooms, and 28 fireplaces. For recreation, the First Family can enjoy a tennis court, jogging track, swimming pool, movie theater, and bowling alley, all without leaving the comfort of their very famous home.*

In this paragraph, the topic was introduced in the first sentence. The following sentences describe what the White House looks like from the outside, the structure of the inside, and the recreational features of the building. Each of these details helps give the reader a clear picture of the topic.

Inferences

Sometimes, writers come right out and directly state everything they want readers to know. Other times, a writer will make suggestions about a person, place, event, or object without directly stating the information. To gain a complete understanding of the passage, readers have to read between the lines and construct meaning about the information in the text. An educated guess based on clues in the passage is an **inference**.

To make an inference, consider

- clues and hints in the passage.
- your own prior knowledge.
- observations.
- details in the text.

Making inferences is similar to drawing conclusions, which was discussed in a Chapter 5.

When readers make inferences, they recognize ideas that are implied.

> *Elliot showed his little brother around the school, making sure he would be able to find his locker, classrooms, and most importantly, the cafeteria.*

What information is implied in this sentence? Based on what we read, what we already know, and what makes logical sense, we can infer several things:

> *Elliot's brother is unfamiliar with the school.*

> *Elliot's brother is a new student.*

> *Elliot already attends the school.*

These ideas were not directly stated. However, if we read between the lines, we can infer that they are most likely true.

TIP

Keep in mind that inferences are not random, wild guesses. They are based on information that you have been given as well as what you already know. Inferences are *logical* conclusions.

At times, you will have to make inferences to determine different things about a passage, such as the main idea, purpose, tone, or point of view. You will have to pay attention to the details in the text to infer this information.

To gain a complete understanding of the text, readers may have to make **multiple inferences** by considering information from various parts of the text. This requires readers to think about their purpose for reading, evaluate the importance of ideas and details, then decide what information is key to understanding what the writer wants them to know about the passage.

For example, suppose you are reading a passage describing how to make a birdhouse. Based on the purpose of the text, you know that it is essential to find the steps necessary to complete the project. If you came across information describing why birds migrate in the winter, you could categorize these facts as being unimportant to the purpose of this particular passage. If you came across information telling you to first measure a piece of wood, you would know that this detail is essential in understanding the text.

BOOST

Did you know that about 71% of people who take the GED® test have already reached at least grade 10? Comedian Bill Cosby left high school in grade 10, passed his GED, then went on to Temple University. In fact, one in ten college freshmen earned their GED credential before arriving on campus!

Readers also might need to consider information from various parts of the text to make strong predictions. Think of each piece of information as a piece to a jigsaw puzzle. The more pieces you have, the better equipped you will be to predict what the finished puzzle will look like. Consider each piece of information as it relates to what you have already read. Then, use this combination of ideas to infer what is likely to happen next in the text.

Considering all the pieces of information in a passage can also be helpful in making inferences about the author. What authors say, as well as what they do not say, can help readers recognize their attitudes, beliefs, biases, prejudgments, and opinions about the topic.

Four bands performed at the school's Winter Wonderland Formal. The ultimate hip-hop band Sticks and Stones rocked the crowd first. Nearly every student was on the dance floor the entire time they played. The drumbeat of their signature hit "Keep Movin'" undoubtedly stuck in everyone's heads for days. After their set, the bands Golden Child, Harvey's Dudes, and Stumped also played.

Which inference could be made about the passage?
a. The author is the drummer in a hip-hop band.
b. Sticks and Stones was the audience's favorite musical group.
c. Nearly all the students attended the Winter Wonderland Formal.
d. Most students at the Winter Wonderland Formal prefer hip-hop music.
e. The author believes Sticks and Stones was the best band at the dance.

The author's opinion about the bands is obvious. You could probably read between the lines and infer that the author really enjoyed the performance by Sticks and Stones. Think about all the words and details he or she included when talking about the band. Then, think about what he or she *didn't* say; the author only quickly mentioned the other bands, without giving any information about the bands or their performances. Choice **e** is the best answer.

Quiz

Now that you've had a chance to review some of the skills needed to comprehend nonfiction, read each of the following passages, then choose the one best answer to each question.

Directions: Choose the *one best answer* to each question.

Questions 1 through 5 refer to the following passage.

What Is Included in a Healthy Diet?

Most people recognize the importance of a healthy lifestyle. Part of this includes enjoying a balanced diet. Each day, people need to eat foods from each food group to
(5) be sure they are getting the benefits offered by each type of food.

It is recommended that people enjoy between six and 11 servings of food from the grain food group. These foods include
(10) bread, rice, pasta, and cereal. Those made from whole grains offer the most health benefits. Enjoying whole grain toast for breakfast, a sandwich on a wheat pita for lunch, and whole wheat pasta for dinner are
(15) ways to ensure that plenty of servings of these foods have found their way onto our plates.

We all know the benefits of eating plenty of fruits and vegetables, but do we
(20) really get enough every day? It is recommended that people enjoy three to five servings of vegetables and three to four servings of fruit every day. That may sound like a lot, but whipping up a fruit smoothie
(25) at the beginning of the day, having veggies and dip as a snack, and adding fresh berries to a yogurt parfait for dessert are ways to think outside of the box—a box of fruit snacks, that is.
(30) Getting enough protein doesn't have to mean eating two to three burgers each day. Did you know that beans, eggs, and nuts are considered protein as well? Sure, a burger, fish, chicken, or steak would be great at
(35) lunch or dinner, but including eggs at breakfast or a handful of almonds in the afternoon can cut down on the amount of

meat in your diet, while still guaranteeing the protein your body needs.
(40) We all know the importance of dairy for strong teeth and bones. But don't feel that you have to drown yourself in skim milk to get your two to three servings a day. Remember that fruit and yogurt parfait?
(45) That's a yummy way to get a full serving of dairy. And how about the grilled cheese sandwich on wheat for lunch? Cheese is another way to get some dairy into your diet.

Eating a balance of food from each
(50) group is essential to staying healthy and feeling your best. Remember to mix it up. Try new things and be sure to get the servings you need each day.

1. Which statement from the passage is an opinion?
   a. Most people recognize the importance of a healthy lifestyle.
   b. Those made from whole grains offer the most health benefits.
   c. That's a yummy way to get a full serving of dairy.
   d. Cheese is another way to get some dairy into your diet.
   e. Try new things and be sure to get the servings you need each day.

2. Which organizational structure is used in the passage?
   a. sequence
   b. classification
   c. cause and effect
   d. problem and solution
   e. compare and contrast

3. What is the main idea of the passage?
   a. We need to include plenty of dairy in our diets.
   b. Most foods can be grouped into five basic types.
   c. A balanced diet is an important part of a healthy lifestyle.
   d. There are creative ways to be sure we eat the right nutrients.
   e. Many people do not eat enough fruits and vegetables each day.

4. Which detail supports the main idea of the third paragraph?
   a. A fruit smoothie can help us get enough servings of fruit.
   b. A box of fruit snacks offers an entire serving of fresh fruit.
   c. We all know the benefits of eating plenty of fruits and vegetables.
   d. We need between six and nine servings of vegetables and fruits daily.
   e. Berry and yogurt parfaits are one way to get enough dairy in our diets.

5. Which choice best summarizes the passage?
   a. A balanced diet includes plenty of grains, fruits and vegetables, dairy, and protein to help us stay healthy. These foods can be incorporated into our diets in creative ways throughout the day.
   b. Protein and dairy are important foods that come from many sources. Meats, nuts, and eggs offer our bodies the protein we need, while milk, yogurt, and cheese give us dairy for strong bones and teeth.
   c. Eating the right kinds of foods is important to staying healthy. Exercise, plenty of sleep, and eating a balanced diet ensure that we have enough energy every day as well as the nutrients we need to build muscles.
   d. Each day, we need six to 11 servings of grains, especially whole grains. We can get these nutrients from breads, cereals, rice, and pasta. Including these foods at every meal will ensure that we get enough of them.
   e. Most people recognize the importance of a healthy lifestyle. Part of this includes enjoying a balanced diet. Each day, people need to eat foods from each food group to be sure they are getting the benefits offered by each type of food.

Questions 6 through 10 refer to the following passage.

What Types of Jobs Are Available?
Currently, Fairhaven Fine Furnishings has a job opening available in the warehouse. Daily job requirements include unloading trucks of furniture and accessories delivered
(5) by the manufacturers, organizing these items in the warehouse, locating and preparing items to fill customer orders, and loading these items onto our company's trucks for delivery. This job requires
(10) employees to be able to lift at least 100 pounds, operate a forklift, and demonstrate

exceptional record-keeping abilities, as maintaining accurate inventory is of utmost importance. This job offers many

(15) opportunities for future advancement within the company. Many of Fairhaven's current management team members began their careers working in the warehouse. This is a full-time position, paying $17.75 per hour.

(20) Health insurance, including vision and dental benefits, will be available after 90 days, assuming the employee receives an acceptable performance evaluation at that point.

(25) Fairhaven Fine Furnishings also has openings available for a data entry clerk and a receptionist. Both positions require exceptional computer skills, and applicants will need to demonstrate adequate abilities

(30) prior to being hired. The receptionist must also have excellent communication and customer service skills, as he or she will be responsible for answering phone calls and greeting customers as they enter our

(35) showroom. Likewise, the data entry clerk must demonstrate strong communication skills, as this position requires interacting with company representatives from our various departments as well as

(40) representatives from each of the companies that provide our products. However, the data entry clerk will not be communicating directly with Fairhaven's customers. The receptionist position is full-time and pays

(45) $10.50 per hour. The data entry position is 20 hours per week and pays $12.35 per hour. Both positions include health insurance benefits following an acceptable 90-day performance evaluation. The company will

(50) also contribute toward vision and dental benefits, making a greater contribution toward these benefits for full-time employees than those working part-time.

Applicants for any of these positions

(55) must first submit a completed resume, including work and salary history, and a list of three professional references. After these documents have been reviewed by a department manager, qualified applicants

(60) will be contacted for a telephone interview. The final step in the hiring process will be a personal interview with our hiring team.

6. Based on the passage, which of these statements is a fact?
   a. Fairhaven Fine Furnishings would be a great place to work.
   b. The receptionist position is better suited for a woman than a man.
   c. All the available positions offer some health insurance benefits.
   d. The phone interview is the most important step in the hiring process.
   e. Working in the warehouse would be more difficult than doing data entry.

7. What is the organizational structure of the first paragraph?
   a. sequential
   b. description
   c. cause and effect
   d. problem and solution
   e. compare and contrast

8. Which is true about the second and third paragraphs?
   a. The second paragraph uses classification to group similar ideas.
   b. The steps in the application process are listed in a random order.
   c. Signal words indicate a cause and effect structure in the paragraphs.
   d. The third paragraph introduces a problem, then lists possible solutions.
   e. Two job positions are compared and contrasted in the second paragraph.

9. Which inference can best be made, based on the information in the passage?
- **a.** The data entry clerk is the most important position.
- **b.** Warehouse employees are valued very highly within the company.
- **c.** The company is likely to hire the first applicants for each of the jobs.
- **d.** The receptionist position will be the most difficult for the company to fill.
- **e.** Part-time employees deserve less compensation than full-time employees.

10. What is the main idea of the third paragraph?
- **a.** Some applicants will be invited to interview in person.
- **b.** There are several steps involved in the hiring process.
- **c.** Department managers will contact qualified applicants by phone.
- **d.** Only the most qualified applicants will meet with the hiring team.
- **e.** Applicants must first submit a resume with work and salary history.

Answers

1. c. Not everyone would agree that a certain food is *yummy*, which makes this statement an opinion. The other answer choices all include statements that could be proven. Most people do know that a healthy lifestyle is important, and the information about whole grains and cheese could be verified in a health or science textbook.

2. b. The types of foods needed to stay healthy are classified by similarities. Each of the food groups discussed is a category. Information about the types of food in each category, as well as the number of servings needed daily, is included in that section of the text.

3. c. The importance of a balanced diet is the main point that the author wants readers to understand. Including plenty of dairy is a detail that supports the main idea. While it is true that most foods can be grouped into five basic types, this is not the main point of the passage.

4. a. Choice **d** states the main idea of the third paragraph, and the statement that fruit smoothies are one way to get enough servings of fruit supports this idea. Fruit snacks are mentioned in the passage, but nothing is said about them actually offering a serving of fruit. Choice **c** is also a statement from the passage; however, it does not support the main idea. Because choice **e** focuses on getting enough dairy, it does not support the idea of eating enough fruits and vegetables.

5. a. Choice **a** restates the main idea and the most important details from the passage. While choice **e** includes the main idea and some pertinent facts, it copies the exact words of the author. Remember, a summary restates or paraphrases the most important ideas in your own words. Choice **b** summarizes the third and fourth paragraphs, while choice **d** summarizes the second paragraph. The information in choice **c** is true; however, it includes information that was not mentioned in the paragraph.

6. c. By reading the job descriptions, we can prove that each position offers insurance benefits. Because the statement can be verified, it is a fact. Not everyone would agree with the other four answer choices, so they are opinions.

7. b. The topic of this paragraph is the warehouse employee position. This topic is introduced in the beginning of the paragraph, then the remainder of the sentences describe the position. The requirements, hours, salary, and benefits are all explained. The order of the information is not important, there is not a problem to discuss, no events result in the occurrence of other events, and the position is not compared to any other job opportunities.

8. e. The words *both* and *likewise* indicate ways in which the two jobs are similar. *However*, *on the other hand*, and *greater* point out differences between the two positions. The third paragraph uses a sequential organizational structure, listing the steps in the order in which they will occur. *First*, *after*, and *final* are clues of the structure used in this paragraph.

9. b. Several clues help you read between the lines in this passage. Notice that the warehouse employee receives a much higher salary and more benefits than the others. Also, the passage states that the warehouse job "offers many opportunities for future advancement" and that "many of Fairhaven's current management team members began their careers working in the warehouse." Such advancement is not mentioned for either of the other available positions. These hints indicate that warehouse employees are valued highly within the company.

10. b. The main idea of this paragraph is implied rather than directly stated. Readers are able to infer this information by reading the entire paragraph. Although it is not the main idea, readers can also infer the idea that only the most qualified applicants will meet with the hiring team in person because the other steps seem to narrow down the field to only those best suited for the job. Choices **a**, **c**, **d**, and **e** are supporting details.

In this chapter, you learned several strategies to help you better comprehend nonfiction reading materials:

1. The main idea is the central message of a passage. Supporting details help to strengthen readers' understanding of the main idea.

2. To summarize is to restate the most important information in your own words. Be sure to think about the main idea and the most important details when creating a summary.

3. Writers include both facts and opinions to express their ideas. Facts are provable and can be verified; opinions tell someone's personal thoughts or ideas, may vary from one person to another, and cannot be verified.

4. Organizational structure refers to the way ideas are arranged in a passage. Common structures include sequence, cause and effect, compare and contrast, problem and solution, classification, and description.

5. When sequence is used to organize a passage, ideas may be listed in time order or in order of importance. Writers may choose to begin with either the most important or least important idea.

6. A cause and effect structure points out how ideas or events are related. A cause is the reason another event occurs; an effect is the result of one or more causes.

7. To compare is to show how ideas, events, or objects are similar; to contrast is to point out ways in which the topics are different. A compare and contrast structure focuses on these similarities and differences.

8. A problem and solution structure introduces a problem, then discusses one or more possible ways to solve the problem.

9. When a writer uses classification as the organizational structure, he or she groups similar ideas together in categories.

10. A description introduces a topic, then provides information and details to explain the topic to readers.

11. To make an inference means to read between the lines and determine what the writer is telling readers without directly stating that information.

12. At times, readers will need to make multiple inferences to fully understand a passage. This may require putting together bits of information located throughout the text to figure out what the writer wants readers to understand.

CHAPTER

7

▶ TIPS AND STRATEGIES

CHAPTER SUMMARY
This chapter covers GED® reading tips and strategies that will help you be successful on exam day. You'll learn how to read each kind of passage effectively and efficiently, how to select and eliminate answers, and how to manage your time during the test. This chapter also contains stress management strategies for the days before and the day of the real test.

Throughout this book, you've learned about the types of materials you'll find on the GED® Language Arts, Reading test, and you've reviewed the strategies that will help you best comprehend the passages. In this chapter, we discuss some general tips for taking the test as well as some useful tips for each type of passage you will read.

Reading the Passages

Keep in mind that you will be reading several passages on the test. Seventy-five percent of the reading material will be fiction, including prose, drama, and poetry. Twenty-five percent of the material will be nonfiction.

Pay Attention to the Purpose Question

As you already know, each passage is preceded by a purpose question. This question is printed in bold and is there to give you a purpose and focus as you read. Use this question to your benefit. Read it carefully, and think about what you might read about in the passage.

Suppose the following is one of the purpose questions on your test:

Who Is Knocking?

How can this help you? Well, before you even begin reading, you know that in the passage, you will read about someone knocking. Because the purpose question doesn't tell you who that is, you know you need to look for that information as you read. For some reason, this is going to be important for you to know.

> The purpose question is just there to provide a focus for your reading; you will not have to answer this question.

Read the Questions First

Another way to help you focus on important information as you read a passage is to take a quick look at the questions *before* you begin reading. This will help you know what information to look for in the passage.

1. How does the author feel about the topic?

By reading the questions ahead of time, you know you need to look for words and details that offer clues about the author's attitude toward the subject matter. This could help focus your attention as you read and possibly save time in the long run.

First Scan, Then Read

You may find it helpful to quickly scan the passage to identify the main idea, then go back and read the passage carefully. Knowing the main idea first can help you identify supporting details as you read. This also lets you know what information you should be looking for when you read the passage slowly and critically the second time.

Read Carefully

Make sure you read slowly and carefully enough to catch every single detail. You may be a master at skimming a passage to simply get the gist of it, but now is not the time to practice that skill. Really focus on the material and think about what you are reading.

Use Context Clues

Don't get upset if you come across an unfamiliar word in a passage. Use what you have learned about context clues to figure out the meaning. Try doing the following:

- Notice how the word is used in the sentence.
- Read the surrounding sentences.
- Look for hints such as synonyms, antonyms, examples, and definitions.
- Think about what would make sense in the context of the passage.

To correctly answer the questions, it is imperative that you completely understand each passage.

Notice Important Details

As you read, pay attention to words, phrases, and details that seem to be important to the meaning of the passage. Be on the lookout for the information listed here:

- key words
- names of real people
- names of characters
- names of locations
- dates
- headings
- specific details
- clues about mood or tone
- hints about the theme
- point of view

TIP

If a word is in *italics* or CAPS or is underlined or **bold**, it is probably important. Pay close attention to this information.

Read Everything

As you read, you may come across information that is set off in brackets. These are explanatory notes that can provide valuable information.

Information in brackets [such as these] can be helpful in selecting the best answer.

It may be tempting to skip over the information in the brackets, especially if you're beginning to feel the time crunch. Don't skip anything. Be sure to read all the information you've been given. It may be there for a good reason.

Classify Information

As you read, be sure to recognize the difference between the main idea and supporting details. Also, be sure to recognize whether a statement is a fact or an opinion. Classifying statements correctly can help you completely understand the passage and mentally organize the ideas you have read.

Don't Forget the Visuals

Any time a passage includes visual displays, pay close attention to them! They are probably there for a reason and often include extremely valuable information that will deepen your understanding of the passage. Visual aids that you might find include the following:

- maps
- charts
- graphs
- diagrams
- illustrations
- photographs

Read the titles, labels, and captions as well as the information contained within the visuals themselves.

Reading the Questions

There will be a total of 40 multiple-choice questions on the test. Each question will be followed by several answer choices. The questions will be arranged in order from easiest to most difficult.

Read the Passage Completely

Some people find it helpful to read the questions before reading the passage. That's great; however, you need to read the passage completely before trying to actually *answer* the questions, even if the questions appear to be simple. Most of the questions will require you to understand the entire passage completely in order to correctly answer them. Remember, this is not the time to assume that you know what the passage is about. Read the entire text carefully, then answer the questions.

Carefully Read the Questions

This may seem obvious, but it is vital that you read each question carefully and make sure you completely understand exactly what is being asked. In fact, read each question twice. How can you select the correct answer if you misread or do not understand the question?

Which of the following is least likely to occur next?

Suppose you read this question too quickly. You might miss the word *least*. This one simple word completely changes the question. Overlooking one word in a question could cause you to select the wrong answer choice.

Also, it may be tempting to assume that you know what the question is asking, especially if several similar questions are grouped together and you're feeling rushed for time. But remember—just because it would be logical for a certain question to come next, there's no guarantee that it will.

Pay Attention to Line Numbers

Some questions may refer to line numbers in the passage. Be sure to refer back to the passage and reread the information in that line again. It is important to understand the words and information in the correct context.

> *What is the meaning of the word* buffet *in line 17?*

You're probably familiar with the word *buffet* and could easily give a definition. But, this word does have several meanings. Without reading line 17, how will you know which meaning is correct?

> *(17) Heavy raindrops and hail continued to buffet the tiny cabin throughout the night.*

Now that you've read the word in the correct context, you will be able to select the appropriate meaning.

Pay Attention to Information in the Question

The question itself may offer essential information that you will need in order to select the best answer choice. Synthesis questions, for example, require you to combine information provided in the question with information in the passage.

Other questions may refer to a specific quotation or section of the passage. If so, there's a pretty good chance that the answer can be found in or near that section. The reference is there for a reason.

TIP

Any information that is offered within a question is important! It would not be there if you didn't need it.

Selecting the Best Answer

You know all the reasons why test takers should read the passages and questions carefully. Now comes the part that makes all the difference: selecting the best answer. When all is said and done, this is the part of the test that matters most. To do well on the GED, it is essential that you select the best possible answer to each question.

Try to Answer the Question before Reading the Choices

As soon as you finish reading the question, think about what the best answer would be. Then, see if your answer is among the choices listed. If so, there's a good chance that it is correct, but don't mark the answer right away. Read all the choices first to be sure your answer is really the most complete option.

Read Every Choice

As you read the answer choices, you may determine that the first choice looks really great. But don't stop there! Read every single choice, no matter how wonderful any one of them appears to be. You may find that one of the first answers looks good but that the last one is even better.

Read Each Choice Carefully

Remember how important it is to be sure you read every single word in a question? The same holds true for reading each answer choice. Read each choice slowly and carefully, paying attention to every word. Take the time to read each answer choice twice before making your selection. Slight differences in wording can make one answer choice better than the others.

Use the Information in the Passage

Make sure that you choose an answer based solely on the information in the passage. You may already know a lot about the topic, which is great; however, the correct answers are in the passage. This test is not asking about what you knew before you read the material; it only wants to find out whether you are able to identify the correct information in this text.

Avoid Careless Mistakes

There will probably be answers you know right off the bat. Don't rush on these. Even if a question appears to be easy, read the question and answer choices carefully before making your selection. Careless mistakes can lower your score.

Watch Out for Absolutes

If certain words are found in answer choices, they should catch your attention. Look for words such as these:

- always
- never
- forever
- every

It is unlikely that the correct answer choice includes these inflexible words. Very few things are *always* true or *never* occur. Be suspicious if an answer choice suggests otherwise.

Pay Attention to Except and Not

Be sure you read every word in a question and pay close attention to the words *except* and *not*. It is easy to overlook these words by reading too quickly, and they completely change the question.

One trick for correctly answering these questions is to cover *except* or *not*, read the question, then look for the answer choice that does *not* belong.

Read Each Question for What It Is

Have you ever read a test question and wondered, *"What is this* really *asking?"* It can be easy to read too much into a question. Try not to do that on this test. The good news is, there are no trick questions on the GED. Just pay attention to what is being asked and select the best answer.

Choose the Best Answer

As you look through all the answer choices, you may find that more than one could be correct. Make sure that the answer you choose *most completely* answers the question. Just because a statement is true or looks like an acceptable choice does not mean it is the *best* answer. Carefully evaluate each choice before making a selection. Also, make sure your choice is the best answer *based on the passage*, not based on your own assumptions or beliefs.

TIP

Tempting answer choices are often listed before the best answer choice. Read all the answers carefully and make sure you completely understand each option before selecting the best response.

Read the Question Again

After you have selected your answer, read the question one more time. Make sure that your choice actually answers the question that was asked. Read the question, the appropriate section of the passage, and any visual aids, then read your answer choice. Does your answer make sense? If so, great! If not, now is your chance to try again.

Trust Your Instincts

Did you know that your first answer is usually correct? If you know that you have carefully read the passage and each answer choice, you have probably selected your best choice.

You may have time at the end of the test to look back over some of your answers. Unless you find an obvious mistake that you are certain about, don't change your answers. Research has shown that your first answer is usually right.

Answer Every Question

Make sure you do not leave any answers blank. Any question that is not answered is considered wrong, so take your best guess. There is no guessing penalty, so it is better to guess than to not answer a question.

BOOST

If you have been diagnosed as having a learning disability or physical handicap, you may be entitled to special accommodations for taking the GED® test. Be sure to check with the testing center you will be attending ahead of time to find out what, if any, documentation you might need to provide.

Eliminating Answer Choices

There may be times when you have no idea which answer choice is correct, and your only option is to take your best guess. In this situation, it is important to eliminate as many incorrect answer choices as possible, then select among those that remain.

Think of it this way: If you randomly choose one of the five answer choices, you have a 1 in 5 chance of getting it right. That's a 20% chance. Not bad, but definitely not in your best interest.

Suppose you are able to eliminate one of the answer choices. Now, you have a 1 in 4 chance of guessing correctly. Your odds just increased to 25%. Eliminate two choices and you have a 1 in 3 chance of answering correctly. This 33% chance of getting the answer right is much better than what you started with.

Now, eliminate three incorrect choices, and you get to choose between the two remaining answers; one is right, and the other is wrong. This gives you a 1 in 2 chance of guessing correctly. You've just improved your odds to 50%. Now, your random guess is much more likely to be the correct answer.

A few hints follow on how to make your best guess. These are only hints and will not work every single time. It is always better to use what you know and select the best answer based on the passage. Use these hints if your only option is making a random guess.

Look for Similar Answers

If you find that two of the answer choices are almost exactly the same, with the exception of a few words, eliminate the other answers and select between these two.

Also Look for Opposite Answers

You may notice that two of the answer choices are opposites.

Which is true about the duck-billed platypus?
a. It lays eggs.
b. It is a bird.
c. It does not lay eggs.
d. It is a vegetarian.
e. It is native to Africa.

Notice that choices a and c are opposites, and obviously, both cannot be correct. So, you can automatically eliminate at least one of these answers. In this case, choice a happens to be correct. However, keep in mind that in another question, it is possible that both of the opposite answers could be wrong.

Get Rid of Extremes

Sometimes one answer may seem very different from the rest. In this case, eliminate the extreme answer.

Where did the story take place?
a. Alabama
b. Florida
c. Georgia
d. Mississippi
e. Paraguay

The answer choices here include four southern states and a foreign country. Paraguay seems a little extreme among the other choices in the list. If you are going to try to eliminate an answer so that you can make your best guess, Paraguay might be the most logical choice to eliminate.

Look for Grammatical Hints

Some questions may require you to choose the answer choice that correctly completes a sentence. Look for any choices that do not fit grammatically and eliminate these. For example, if the beginning of the sentence is written in past tense and an answer choice is in present tense, there's a good chance that the answer is incorrect.

If you are asked to choose a missing word or to identify a word with the same meaning, eliminate any choices that are a different part of speech.

The attorney was late for the meeting and asked us to brief her quickly on what had taken place so far.

What best tells the meaning of *brief* in the sentence?
a. for a short time
b. concise without detail
c. to summarize in writing
d. a synopsis of a document
e. to give necessary information

In the sentence, *brief* is a verb, so the correct answer will also be a verb. Choices **a** and **b** are adjectives, and choice **d** is a noun. These can be eliminated, leaving only answers **c** and **e**, which are both verbs. In this case, **e** is the best choice.

Keeping Track of Time

Remember that this is a timed test. You will have 65 minutes to read the passages and answer 40 multiple-choice questions. Being aware of how much time has passed and how much time remains can make a tremendous difference in your overall performance.

Wear a Watch

Be sure to wear a watch on the day of the test. Check the time as the test begins and figure out the time at which the test will end. The test administrator will probably update you on how much time remains throughout the test. However, it's a good idea to be able to check for yourself.

> **TIP**
>
> Don't wear a watch that has a calculator. If you're taking the math portion of the GED® test on the same day, you may not be allowed to wear your timepiece.

Pace Yourself

Let's do the math. To answer 40 questions in 65 minutes, you'll need to spend an average of about one and a half minutes on each question. That's 10 questions every 15 minutes. This includes reading the passages. That means you should have completed:

- 10 questions in the first 15 minutes
- 20 questions in the first half hour
- 30 questions in 45 minutes
- 40 questions by the end of one hour

If after 15 minutes you have not finished the first 10 questions, try to work a little more quickly. If you're ahead of schedule, you can slow down a bit if you feel rushed, or you can relax with the confidence that there will be time to look over the test when you're done.

Don't Rush

Remember the old saying "Slow and steady wins the race"? Yes, there is a time limit. Yes, you need to pace yourself. However, if you rush, you'll be more likely to make mistakes. Work quickly, but most important, work carefully.

> *It's better to answer some of the questions and get them right than to answer most of the questions and get them wrong.*

Keep an eye on your watch, but keep your focus on doing your best.

TIP

Most people who have not passed the GED test actually had the knowledge needed to pass. So what was the problem? They ran out of time. Don't let this happen to you! Pace yourself, monitor the time, and keep moving.

Use Your Time Wisely

Keep in mind that you have an average of 90 seconds per question. Don't spend too much time trying to select a single answer. If a question has you stumped, take your best guess and move on. You can always come back later if you have extra time at the end. Wasting time on one tricky question can prevent you from having time to answer another that you might think is a breeze.

TIP

Sometimes, if you skip a tough question and come back to it later, you will find it easier to answer the second time around. Information and clues in other questions may help you figure out the best answer.

Wrap Things Up at the End

You already know the importance of keeping an eye on the time. If you find that there are only a couple of minutes left and you have not yet finished the test, start guessing. Any answer that is left blank will automatically be marked wrong. Go ahead and take a stab at any remaining questions; quickly get an answer marked for every test item. At this point, what have you got to lose? You may or may not get them right, but at least you tried, and as previously noted, there is no guessing penalty.

Tips for Prose Fiction Passages

Prose fiction passages involve imaginary people and events. On the test, you will read at least one passage written before 1920, at least one written between 1920 and 1960, and at least one written since 1960.

Make Inferences

Often in fiction passages, the author intentionally leaves out some information. This requires readers to make inferences about the plot, characters, or setting. Use the information that is given or implied to fill in the blanks. For example, you can infer what type of person a character is by paying attention to what other characters say or think about him. You can put together information about the sights, sounds, and smells described in a story to infer the setting.

> *As Maxwell stepped outside, he noticed the sounds of the cows mooing in the distance and could make out the silhouette of the barn on the opposite side of the field. This was nothing like the city he was used to.*

What is the setting of the story?
a. a barn
b. a big city
c. a farm
d. a zoo
e. a small town

The writer mentions a city, but this is not the setting. Because we know that Maxwell hears cows and can see a barn on the other side of the field, we can infer that he is on a farm (choice **c**). If the barn were the setting, he would be in it or near it; it would not be in the distance.

Notice Names

Pay close attention to names of people and places as well as to dates and key words. These are often important to remember if you are going to accurately understand the story.

Pay Attention to Details

Details can help you determine many things about a story. This information is invaluable in answering questions about the plot, conflicts, mood, point of view, and theme. If you get to a question about one of these and are unsure of the answer, look back in the passage and see what insight the details can offer.

Tips for Poetry

At least one of the passages you will read will be a poem. The poems you read on the test may be humorous or serious. Don't worry about them being overly complicated or drowning in symbolism, but do keep in mind that reading poetry is different than reading prose.

Read the Title

When you are in a hurry, it may be tempting to skip the title of a poem. How important can it be anyway, right? Actually, the title may offer a little insight about the topic and theme. This information could prove to be quite useful.

Read Slowly

As you know, poetry is not arranged in the same way as prose. A single sentence may be divided between several lines. In fact, the entire poem might be comprised of a single sentence. As you read, notice where each sentence begins and ends. This will help you see where each idea begins and ends. Read slowly and focus on each complete sentence, regardless of how it is arranged in the poem.

TIP

Sometimes words are arranged in a different order in poetry than they would be in prose. This can make it difficult to determine meaning. Try rearranging the words into an order that makes more sense.

Read Aloud

Reading a poem aloud can be helpful. However, you won't be able to talk during the actual test. As you study and practice, try reading aloud. On test day, focus on the sound and rhythm of the words as if you were reading aloud.

Read It Again

It can be very helpful to read a poem at least twice. The first time, read it for the literal meaning. The second time, read it for deeper or figurative meaning. If you are still not sure what the poet is trying to say, read it again.

Also, as you read, be sure to identify each of the following elements:

- the speaker
- rhyme
- rhythm
- figurative language

Tips for Drama

As you know, drama is written to be performed rather than read. Keep in mind that the dialogue and stage directions will provide all the writer's ideas.

Read Everything
Remember that the stage directions and explanatory notes offer important information. These may be located in parentheses or brackets. Don't skip them. They can prove to be extremely helpful in completely understanding the setting as well as the characters' actions, emotions, and motivations.

Visualize the Play
As you read drama, imagine that you are watching the action on a stage or movie screen. Picture the characters, imagine each of their voices, and create an image of the setting in your head. Now you are able to see and hear the story as it takes place. The more of your senses you involve, the better you will understand what is happening.

Question Yourself
As you read drama, ask yourself the following questions to monitor your understanding of the script:

- What is the setting of this scene?
- Who are the characters in this part of the play?
- What are the characters discussing?
- Is the meaning of their conversation literal or figurative?
- What inferences can be made about the characters' motivations?
- How do the characters respond to one another?
- What does the conversation reveal about the characters' relationships?
- What do the characters' relationships reveal about them or the situation?

If you are unsure of any of the answers, look back through the text and clarify anything you do not fully understand.

Tips for Nonfiction Passages

The purpose of the nonfiction passages may be to entertain, inform, or persuade readers. Regardless of their purpose, these passages are based on actual people, topics, or events and will offer information, facts, and details about the topic.

Notice Details
Watch for details such as statistics, dates, names, events, section headings, and key words that are included in the passage. You may see these again when you get to the questions.

Pay Attention to Descriptive Language
Descriptive language can offer clues about an author's views on the topic. After you find the main idea, begin looking for language, facts, and details that support the author's point of view.

Look for Evidence
Keep in mind that each paragraph of a nonfiction passage will have a main idea. The rest of the paragraph will include details to support the main idea. As you read, search for this evidence. Facts, examples, descriptions, and other information that helps explain the main idea are essential to comprehending the text and will probably be the subject of at least some of the questions.

Draw Your Own Conclusions
Some types of nonfiction passages, such as commentaries, will include many opinions, which vary greatly from one person to the next. Pay attention to any summaries or descriptions of the work, then use details in

the text to make inferences and create your own judgments about the material.

Preparing for the Test

Like so many things, the key to doing well on the GED is preparation. You're already on the right track by reading these chapters. A few other tips to help you prepare are discussed in this section.

Practice, Practice, Practice

Taking a practice test, such as the ones in this book, is a terrific way to be sure you are ready. These practice tests help you in several ways:

- You will know what types of questions to expect.
- You will become comfortable with the format of the test.
- You will learn about your own strengths and weaknesses.
- You will be aware of what you need to study.

As you take the practice tests, pay attention to the types of questions you get right and those that are more challenging. For example, you may find that the questions about main ideas are really easy. That's great! You might also find that you miss a lot of the questions that deal with themes. No problem. Now you know what skills to study.

Create Opportunities for Even More Practice

You probably read different types of passages all the time, either in magazines or newspapers, in novels, or on the Internet. As you read, think about the types of questions you will find on the GED. Then, ask yourself questions about your reading material. For example, you might ask yourself:

- What is the main idea of the passage I just read?
- What details support the main idea?

- What were the conflict and resolution in this story?
- What context clues helped me determine the meanings of unfamiliar words?
- What is the theme (or tone or mood) of the passage?

Another idea is to work with a friend and write questions for each other based on passages you select. You could also summarize passages, underline key words, circle the main idea of each paragraph, and highlight supporting details.

Know Yourself

Figure out what works best for you. For example, not everyone benefits from reading the questions before reading the passage. Some people may find it helpful to scan a passage for the main idea before reading; others may not. Try different strategies as you work through the practice questions and pay attention to which strategies you find most comfortable and most beneficial.

Be Ready the Day before the Test

Being ready mentally and physically can help you do your best on the test. Here are some suggestions:s

- Start studying and preparing in advance; don't plan on cramming for the test in the few days before you are scheduled to take it.
- The day before the test, take a break and relax. Go for a walk, call a friend, or see a movie. Don't stay up late to study.
- Have anything you want to take with you ready ahead of time. Set out your pencils, sweater, watch, or anything else that you need to take to the test location in the morning.
- Make sure you get plenty of sleep the night before the test. If you're concerned that you won't be able to fall asleep, get up extra early the morning before the test. That way, you'll be ready for bed early that evening.

The Big Day

You've studied, you're well rested, and now you're ready to take the GED Language Arts, Reading exam! Now that test day is here, make the most of it.

Get Off to a Good Start

First, set your alarm early enough so that you won't have to rush. Not only will you feel more relaxed and have time to get settled before the test starts, but you also might not be allowed to enter the testing center if you are late. Make sure that being on time is one thing you won't have to worry about.

Then, be sure to eat a well-balanced breakfast. You need to keep your energy up, and you certainly don't want to be distracted by the sound of your stomach growling. If today is going to be a long day of testing, bring a bottle of water, a piece of fruit, or some trail mix to snack on between sessions.

Also, dress in comfortable, layered clothes and bring a sweater. Feeling like your shoes are too tight or being too hot or too cold can be distractions. Do everything you can to be sure you feel great and are on top of your game today!

Keep Your Cool

You've studied, you've practiced, and now you're ready. Don't let your nerves get the best of you. Getting worked up will not help you get your highest possible score. In the overall scheme of things, the GED is just a test. If things don't go as well as you'd hoped today, consider this a practice run. You have three chances in a calendar year to pass the test. Try to stay calm and focus on doing your best.

Carefully Read the Directions

If you are unsure about the directions or what exactly you are supposed to do, be sure to ask the test administrator before you begin the test. He or she cannot help you with specific test questions or vocabulary, but you may be able to get the information you need to clarify the test's instructions.

Clearly Mark Your Answers

Make sure you clearly and completely mark your answer choices. Also, be sure to erase any stray marks or changed answers. These can be misread when the test is electronically scored.

Keep Your Place

Make sure that you mark each answer in the correct spot on the answer sheet. The question number should correspond to the number on the answer sheet. If you decide to skip a question for any reason, be sure to skip the corresponding place on the answer sheet as well. Every ten questions or so, check to see that you are marking the correct bubble for the question you're answering.

Quiz

Directions: Choose the *one best answer* to each question.

Questions 1 through 4 refer to the following passage:

Which Pieces of Art Are the Artist's Best Work?

Local up-and-coming artist Melanie O'Keefe debuted a number of pieces from her collection at the Laurel Oaks Fine Art Museum recently. Attendance at the showing

(5) exceeded expectations and brought a number of renowned art critics to the downtown area. Members of the museum's board of directors were impressed by O'Keefe's display as well as excited about the

(10) attention the show brought to the museum itself.

The most prominent piece in the collection, "Springtime Rain," will remain on display for approximately one year. This
(15) piece depicts two barefoot young children walking through a field of brightly colored wildflowers during a spring rain shower. The artist's use of light creates a warm effect through the mostly overcast sky and gives a
(20) cheerful feeling to the piece, while the softening of each line nearly creates the effect of looking out of a rain-streaked windowpane. Her attention to detail in each brushstroke lends a professional quality to
(25) the work of a relative newcomer in the field.

O'Keefe's signature watercolor piece, "Winter in the City," depicts a cityscape of the early years of our own town, including only a few early model vehicles and several
(30) residents wrapped in heavy coats and scarves, walking along the brick roads. The artist's use of texture and shadow allows museum visitors to feel the chill in the air and hear the sounds of the wind whistling between
(35) the buildings. The use of various shades of grays and blues adds to the depth of the piece while helping to create the feelings of a winter day. The subtle use of white light to illuminate the streetlamps
(40) nearly causes them to pop off the canvas.

The charcoal drawings in the collection drew an impressive amount of attention from visitors, although these works do not display the same quality as her works done
(45) in other mediums. The overall images are pleasant to view but portray an amateur feel. "Cottage on the Shore" was undoubtedly the most memorable piece created in this portion of the show; however, it was the
(50) subject matter rather than the talent of the artist that will remain in the viewers' minds. It is apparent that these are the earliest pieces O'Keefe created.

1. Based on the passage, all the statements below are true about Melanie O'Keefe EXCEPT which one?
   a. She is a relatively new artist.
   b. Painting is her favorite form of art.
   c. Her work was displayed in the museum.
   d. The names of two of her pieces mention seasons.
   e. She is from the same town where the work was shown.

2. Which is true about the writer of the commentary?
   a. The writer enjoys art exhibitions by local artists the best.
   b. The writer is a member of the museum's board of directors.
   c. The writer never likes artwork that includes the use of charcoal.
   d. The writer always prefers watercolor paintings to other art forms.
   e. The writer felt the charcoal drawings were the weakest in the collection.

3. What can be concluded about the artist and her work?
   a. The artist should have used light in the charcoal drawings and the paintings.
   b. The artist included an impressive use of light in all the pieces in the display.
   c. The artist's use of light is one of the prominent aspects of some of her artwork.
   d. The artist's use of light is better in "Winter in the City" than in "Springtime Rain."
   e. The artist's use of light is better in "Springtime Rain" than in "Winter in the City."

4. Which statement can be inferred about the artwork in the exhibit?

    a. "Springtime Rain" was created using paint.

    b. "Winter in the City" was the most recent piece on display.

    c. "Cottage on the Shore" showed use of texture and shadow.

    d. "Springtime Rain" and "Winter in the City" were both watercolors.

    e. "Cottage on the Shore" was the most professional piece on display.

Answers

1. b. Notice that the question includes the word *except*. The answer choices include four statements that are true, based on the passage, and one that is not. While several of the pieces in the exhibit were paintings, nothing in the passage states that this is her favorite form of art. This question is an example of why it is crucial that test takers carefully read every word; had someone overlooked the word *except*, he or she might have been looking for a statement that was true rather than the one statement that was not true.

2. e. Choice **e** is the only one supported by the information in the passage. Choices **c** and **d** might be tempting because the statements contain some truth in regard to this particular art show; the writer does prefer these paintings to the charcoal drawings. However, remember what you read about answers that are absolutes. These choices include the words *never* and *always*. If you needed to eliminate incorrect answer choices, these would be a good place to start. The passage does not suggest that the writer always likes one form of art and never likes another. Remember, very few things *always* or *never* occur.

3. c. The artist's use of light is mentioned in the review of both "Springtime Rain" and "Winter in the City," implying that this is one of the most noticeable or important aspects of these pieces. Suppose you were unsure of which answer choice was correct. Which could be eliminated to help you make a strong guess? Notice that choice **b** includes the word *all*. This word is an absolute that must be carefully considered before selecting this answer. If you needed to get rid of one option, this might be a good one to eliminate. Then, notice that choices **d** and **e** are opposites. Obviously one, if not both, of these can be eliminated. In this case, nothing in the passage indicates that the use of light is better in one piece than it is in the other, so both can be eliminated.

4. a. Here's an example of why readers need to notice details. Without paying attention to the names of each piece of artwork, it would be difficult to know which statements are true about the artist's displays. The passage never directly states that "Springtime Rain" is a painting, but the attention to detail in each brushstroke is mentioned. Beause brushstrokes are used in painting, readers can infer that this piece is a painting. While the writer does mention that the charcoal drawings are the artist's earliest works, he or she does not tell which work is the most recent. The use of texture and shadow, watercolors, and professionalism are mentioned in the passage, but not regarding the pieces named in choices **c**, **d**, and **e**.

In this chapter, you learned a number of tips that will help you do your best on the GED Language Arts, Reading exam:

1. Before you begin reading a passage, be sure to pay attention to the purpose question that precedes the passage as well as the comprehension questions that follow it.

2. Scan the passage first, then read it carefully, noticing important details and mentally organizing the information. Remember to read the information in brackets, the visual aids, and the captions as well.

3. After you read the passage completely, thoroughly read each question, paying close attention to any information stated within the question itself.

4. Try to answer each question before you actually read the answer choices. Then, read each choice carefully, paying close attention to every word, before selecting the best answer based on the passage.

5. After selecting an answer, reread the question to make sure your answer choice is the best fit.

6. Answer every single question, even if it means you have to guess.

7. If you are unsure of which answer to choose, look for options that are similar or are opposites, contain extremes, or have grammatical hints. Then, eliminate as many choices as possible before taking your best guess. Remember, the more options you eliminate, the better your chance of choosing the correct response.

8. Because the GED is a timed test, it is essential that you are aware of the time. Wear a watch, pace yourself, and don't spend too much time on any one question. If you see that time is running out, quickly select an answer for each of the remaining questions.

9. When reading prose fiction passages, be sure to pay attention to details, such as the names of characters or places, and use the ideas that are included in the passage to infer information that the author has not included.

10. Remember that poetry is very different than prose. Be sure to read the title and slowly read the poem at least twice to be sure you comprehend both literal and figurative meanings.

11. Be sure to read everything included in a drama and try to visualize the setting, action, and the characters as you read. Monitor your understanding of the script by asking yourself questions.

12. As you read nonfiction passages, look for evidence that supports the main idea of the passage. Be sure to pay close attention to details, names, dates, statistics, and descriptive language that can enhance your comprehension of the material and help you draw your own conclusions about the topic.

13. Practicing for the test can help you feel prepared, show you important information about your own strengths and weaknesses, and make you aware of the strategies that work best for you.

14. Take a break the day before the test. Don't study too much that day, and be sure to get a good night's sleep.

15. Get up early and have a good breakfast on the morning of the test. Wear comfortable clothes and dress in layers in case the testing center is too warm or too cool for your liking.

16. Read the test directions carefully and ask questions if you need to. When you choose your answer, mark it clearly and completely, making sure that you are writing in the space on the answer key that corresponds to the correct question number.

A Final Word

Whew! Throughout this book, you've reviewed a number of reading comprehension strategies that will help you do your best on the GED® Language Arts, Reading test. In this chapter, you've learned some tips that will help you do your best as you put the comprehension strategies into practice. You are on your way to earning an outstanding score on the test and bringing home the ultimate prize—your GED® credential!

Certainly, remembering all this information and facing the GED® test can be intimidating, but you are taking all the right steps toward doing your best. Review the comprehension strategies until you are comfortable and confident in your abilities with each. Take the practice tests in this book and monitor your own learning. If there are skills you need to brush up on, go back to that section of the book and review the information. When you find skills that you have mastered, give yourself a pat on the back. You've earned it!

Keep the test-taking tips in this chapter in mind any time you take a test, not just the GED® test. Reading passages and answer choices carefully, paying attention to details, and selecting the one best answer choice are great ways to earn a top-notch score on any test. And don't sweat it when you come across a question that seems especially tough. It happens to everyone. Remember to carefully eliminate answer choices and look for grammatical clues before taking a guess. Furthermore, don't waste your time on questions you're just not sure of. Take a deep breath, mark your strongest guess, and move on. You can always come back at the end if time allows.

Remember, you're on the right track. Taking charge of your own learning and being prepared are great first steps toward a successful GED® testing experience. Good luck!

8 ▶ PRACTICE TEST 1

CHAPTER SUMMARY
Here is the first sample test based on the GED® Language Arts, Reading test. After working through the review in Chapters 3 through 7, take this test to see how much your score has improved from the diagnostic test in Chapter 2.

Like the diagnostic test, this practice test mirrors the real GED® Language Arts, Reading test. It consists of 40 multiple-choice questions on reading passages. For this practice test, time yourself. On test day, you will have 65 minutes to complete this part of the exam.

The answer sheet you should use for the multiple-choice questions is on the following page. Then comes the exam itself. After that is the answer key, in which each answer is explained to help you find out why the correct answers are right and why the incorrect answers are wrong.

Practice Test 1

1. ⓐ ⓑ ⓒ ⓓ ⓔ
2. ⓐ ⓑ ⓒ ⓓ ⓔ
3. ⓐ ⓑ ⓒ ⓓ ⓔ
4. ⓐ ⓑ ⓒ ⓓ ⓔ
5. ⓐ ⓑ ⓒ ⓓ ⓔ
6. ⓐ ⓑ ⓒ ⓓ ⓔ
7. ⓐ ⓑ ⓒ ⓓ ⓔ
8. ⓐ ⓑ ⓒ ⓓ ⓔ
9. ⓐ ⓑ ⓒ ⓓ ⓔ
10. ⓐ ⓑ ⓒ ⓓ ⓔ
11. ⓐ ⓑ ⓒ ⓓ ⓔ
12. ⓐ ⓑ ⓒ ⓓ ⓔ
13. ⓐ ⓑ ⓒ ⓓ ⓔ
14. ⓐ ⓑ ⓒ ⓓ ⓔ
15. ⓐ ⓑ ⓒ ⓓ ⓔ
16. ⓐ ⓑ ⓒ ⓓ ⓔ
17. ⓐ ⓑ ⓒ ⓓ ⓔ
18. ⓐ ⓑ ⓒ ⓓ ⓔ
19. ⓐ ⓑ ⓒ ⓓ ⓔ
20. ⓐ ⓑ ⓒ ⓓ ⓔ
21. ⓐ ⓑ ⓒ ⓓ ⓔ
22. ⓐ ⓑ ⓒ ⓓ ⓔ
23. ⓐ ⓑ ⓒ ⓓ ⓔ
24. ⓐ ⓑ ⓒ ⓓ ⓔ
25. ⓐ ⓑ ⓒ ⓓ ⓔ
26. ⓐ ⓑ ⓒ ⓓ ⓔ
27. ⓐ ⓑ ⓒ ⓓ ⓔ
28. ⓐ ⓑ ⓒ ⓓ ⓔ
29. ⓐ ⓑ ⓒ ⓓ ⓔ
30. ⓐ ⓑ ⓒ ⓓ ⓔ
31. ⓐ ⓑ ⓒ ⓓ ⓔ
32. ⓐ ⓑ ⓒ ⓓ ⓔ
33. ⓐ ⓑ ⓒ ⓓ ⓔ
34. ⓐ ⓑ ⓒ ⓓ ⓔ
35. ⓐ ⓑ ⓒ ⓓ ⓔ
36. ⓐ ⓑ ⓒ ⓓ ⓔ
37. ⓐ ⓑ ⓒ ⓓ ⓔ
38. ⓐ ⓑ ⓒ ⓓ ⓔ
39. ⓐ ⓑ ⓒ ⓓ ⓔ
40. ⓐ ⓑ ⓒ ⓓ ⓔ
41. ⓐ ⓑ ⓒ ⓓ ⓔ
42. ⓐ ⓑ ⓒ ⓓ ⓔ
43. ⓐ ⓑ ⓒ ⓓ ⓔ
44. ⓐ ⓑ ⓒ ⓓ ⓔ
45. ⓐ ⓑ ⓒ ⓓ ⓔ
46. ⓐ ⓑ ⓒ ⓓ ⓔ
47. ⓐ ⓑ ⓒ ⓓ ⓔ
48. ⓐ ⓑ ⓒ ⓓ ⓔ
49. ⓐ ⓑ ⓒ ⓓ ⓔ
50. ⓐ ⓑ ⓒ ⓓ ⓔ

Directions: Choose the *one best answer* to each question.

Questions 1 through 7 refer to the following excerpt from a novel.

What Does Daisy Want?

"It is a sad fact that I shall have to return to Geneva tomorrow."

"Well, Mr. Winterbourne," said Daisy, "I think you're horrid!"

(5) "Oh, don't say such awful things!" said Winterbourne, "Just at the last!"

"The last!" cried the young girl. "I call it the first. I have half a mind to leave you here and go straight back to the hotel alone." And

(10) for the next ten minutes, she did nothing but call him horrid.

Poor Winterbourne was confused. No young lady had ever been so upset by the announcement of his movements. His

(15) companion stopped paying any attention to Chillon Castle or the lake. She opened fire upon the mysterious charmer in Geneva whom she seemed to have decided he was hurrying back to see. How did Miss Daisy

(20) Miller know that there was a charmer in Geneva? Winterbourne was quite unable to discover.

And he was divided between being amazed at the quickness of her inference and

(25) being amused at the frankness of her chitchat. She seemed to him an extraordinary mixture of innocence and crudity.

"Does she never allow you more than

(30) three days at a time?" asked Daisy ironically. "Doesn't she give you a vacation in summer? There's no one so hard worked but they can get leave to go off somewhere at this season. I suppose, if you stay another day, she'll

(35) come after you in the boat. Do wait over till Friday, and I will go down to the landing to see her arrive!"

Winterbourne began to think he had been wrong about this young lady's

(40) temperament. If he had missed the personal accent, the personal accent was now making its appearance. It sounded very distinctly in her telling him she would stop "teasing" him if he would promise her to come to Rome in

(45) the winter.

"That's not a difficult promise to make," said Winterbourne. "My aunt has taken an apartment in Rome for the winter. She has already asked me to come and see

(50) her."

"I don't want you to come for your aunt," said Daisy. "I want you to come for me."

Adapted from Henry James, *Daisy Miller*

1. Why is Daisy upset?
   a. She worries that Winterbourne is in love with her.
   b. She tends to be emotional about most things.
   c. She is worried about Winterbourne.
   d. She wants Winterbourne to come to Rome.
   e. She wants Winterbourne to pay more attention to her.

2. Which of the following best describes what Winterbourne thinks about Daisy?
   a. He thinks she is spoiled.
   b. He dislikes the way she talks.
   c. He feels protective toward her.
   d. He is attracted to her passion.
   e. He is startled by her behavior.

3. Based on the excerpt, which description best characterizes the relationship between Winterbourne and Daisy?
   a. tense but caring
   b. competitive and critical
   c. lighthearted but practical
   d. fanciful and dreamlike
   e. indifferent but innocent

4. Based on the excerpt, what is Daisy most likely to do in the future?
   a. apologize to Winterbourne
   b. refuse to see Winterbourne again
   c. return to America at once
   d. visit with Winterbourne's aunt in Rome
   e. make sure that Winterbourne visits her in Rome

5. How does the author depict Daisy?
   a. as a person who is very jealous
   b. as a person with little emotion
   c. as someone who overreacts
   d. as someone with great humor
   e. as a person who is charitable

6. Which of the following best describes what Winterbourne means when he says, "Just at the last" (line 6)?
   a. He is leaving soon.
   b. He and Daisy are breaking up.
   c. He wants their relationship to end.
   d. He feels bitterness toward Daisy.
   e. He wishes Daisy would leave him.

7. In which of the following ways are Daisy and Winterbourne alike?
   a. They are both irritable when upset.
   b. They are both worried about their future.
   c. They are both cutting their trips short.
   d. They are both curious about each other.
   e. They are both disappointed in the outing.

Questions 8 through 13 refer to the following excerpt from a play.

Will They Meet Again?

[The scene is a USO building. A group of soldiers has just entered the room, which has a buffet table and a dance floor. There are several women who are hosts, some who are
(5) young and some who are older.]

Nina: Hi, soldier. Help yourself to something to eat.

Jim: Hi. This is great! Who made all this wonderful food?

(10) Nina: We did, silly. We all pitched in.

Jim [filling his plate]: Well, I never expected this. They just told us there might be some snacks.

Nina: That's not the way we do it here. By
(15) the way, the music is going to start in a bit. Do you like to dance?

Jim: No, not much. I never was any good at it.

Nina: I see. Would you like a lesson? I'm a great dancer.

(20) Jim: Why is it I believe you?

Nina [laughing]: It's because I have an honest face. Hey, my shift is over in 20 minutes. Why don't I check on you then? We can do a little dancing.

(25) [Later Nina finds Jim alone, watching others dance.]

Nina: I told you I'd find you.

Jim [smiling]: So you did! But I'm really not much of a dancer.

(30) Nina: Oh, come on now. [She grabs his hand, and he stands up.] Just copy what I'm doing. Let the music talk to you.

Jim [at first very wooden, but slowly loosening up]: Hey, that is neat. I'm really
(35) having fun.

Nina: I told you so. [Nina starts to sing to the music.] Don't sit under the apple tree with anyone else but me, anyone else but me, anyone else but me . . . no, no, no.

(40)   Jim: You have a nice voice.

Nina [looking up at him, suddenly quite seriously]: When do you ship out?

Jim [Looking taken aback, he stops moving.]: This Wednesday. We all go by ship . . . to

(45)   England and then to the continent.

Nina: Are you frightened?

Jim [tightening his grip on her hand]: Well . . . a little, but it's an important fight. [They stare at each other.]

(50)   Nina [in a low voice]: Be careful. I want to dance with you when you come home.

Jim: Really? You would like to see me again?

Nina: Yes. Here's a lucky penny I have. Will you carry it with you? And then bring it back

(55)   to me?

Jim: Sure. You're swell. [They both laugh and start to dance again.]

8. Based on the information in the excerpt, how would Nina most likely behave on a date?
   a. be too personal
   b. be playful but also serious
   c. be off-putting and indifferent
   d. be secretive but charming
   e. be hard to please

9. Which of the following phrases best describes Jim?
   a. intense and strained
   b. charming and facile
   c. opportunistic and pushy
   d. easygoing and appreciative
   e. glamorous and mysterious

10. Which best describes the mood created in this scene?
   a. serious
   b. suspenseful
   c. lighthearted
   d. intimate
   e. sorrowful

11. Which is the most likely reason that Nina gives Jim a penny?
   a. It is valuable currency.
   b. She no longer needs it.
   c. She wants him to spend it.
   d. She wants him to feel hopeful.
   e. It brings good fortune to the owner.

12. Based on the excerpt, what can be inferred about Nina?
   a. She studies singing.
   b. She wants to find a boyfriend.
   c. She enjoys cheering up soldiers.
   d. She is self-centered.
   e. She likes to be in control.

13. How would the knowledge that Nina is paid to dance with soldiers affect the passage?
   a. It would make her offer to dance seem fake and uncaring.
   b. It would reveal that Nina is just doing her job.
   c. It would question how much of her interest is personal.
   d. It would demonstrate that Nina can be a good friend.
   e. It would explain why she carried a lucky penny with her.

Questions 14 through 18 refer to the following excerpt from a short story.

Will She Land Her Jump?

"Ouch, that hurt," Yolanda said as she ended up falling on her side, yet again.

Her coach, Ellen, spoke. "What happened? You seemed to jump very well,

(5) but then you lost it."

"I just don't seem to be able to get it. I jump high enough, but something happens and I can't land it," Yolanda answered, relacing her skates.

(10) "I know it's not easy, but you can do it. You just have to visualize yourself flying through the air and landing. Think about it. See it in your head. You will get it, Yolanda. I promise you will," Ellen said.

(15) Her coach had been with her since she was a little girl, always encouraging her to try harder, jump higher, achieve more. She was like a family member to her. And like Ellen, Yolanda loved to skate and loved to compete.

(20) She wanted so much to get a chance at Nationals, but she had to land this jump, called an axel. It was required.

"That's it for today, Yolanda. See you tomorrow afternoon," Ellen said. It was

(25) already dark when Yolanda stood outside the arena waiting for her father to pick her up.

"How did it go?" he asked as she climbed into the car.

"I still can't get the jump. Ellen told me

(30) to visualize it. She said I have to see myself doing it in my head before I will do it in reality."

"That sounds smart."

They arrived at home, and they all ate

(35) dinner—she, her father, and her mother. Yolanda turned in early. She fell asleep right away and started to dream. In the dream, she was an eagle that soared through the air and

(40) landed on a small rock in a large lake. It felt wonderful, sailing through the air and landing without any effort.

When she got up the next morning, she thought about her dream, and she started to imagine what it would be like to land the

(45) axel. It was in the back of her mind all day until she reached the arena.

Out on the ice, she felt a thrill of excitement as she picked up the speed needed to jump. Up, up, she went through

(50) the air. She flew and then turned just the right way, landing on one leg and then the other. It was magical.

"I did it! I did it!" she cried as Ellen came to give her a hug.

14. Based on the excerpt, what does Yolanda learn about mastering a jump?
   a. She learns that too much practice can be detrimental.
   b. She learns that she needs greater confidence.
   c. She learns that skating is an art form.
   d. She learns that she needs to practice more.
   e. She learns that she needs a stricter coach.

15. Which of the following best expresses the main idea of the excerpt?
   a. It takes a good deal of stamina to be an ice skater.
   b. Jumps, like life, are difficult to succeed at.
   c. Learning to skate is a lot like learning to swim.
   d. To do something difficult, it may be necessary to internalize it.
   e. A skater and her coach enjoy a close and unique relationship.

16. Which best describes the significance of the dream?
- **a.** It suggests that Yolanda enjoys flying.
- **b.** It suggests that Yolanda will become a great skater.
- **c.** It suggests that Yolanda will succeed with the jump.
- **d.** It shows Yolanda's determination.
- **e.** It shows that Yolanda is upset about her jump.

17. Based on the excerpt, what does Yolanda think of the dream?
- **a.** She sees herself soaring and landing like the eagle.
- **b.** She thinks that she can do anything she wants to do.
- **c.** She worries that she cannot do what the eagle did.
- **d.** She assumes the dream means she will achieve her goal.
- **e.** She wonders at the meaning of the dream.

18. Which phrase best describes Yolanda?
- **a.** realistic and competitive
- **b.** committed and receptive
- **c.** flighty but talented
- **d.** reluctant and nervous
- **e.** confident but practical

Questions 19 through 23 refer to the following poem.

Why Must She Go?

The little Road says, Go,
The little House says, Stay:
And O, it's bonny here at home,
But I must go away.

(5)   The little Road, like me,
Would seek and turn and know;
And forth I must, to learn the things
The little Road would show!

And go I must, my dears,
(10) And journey while I may,
Though heart be sore for the little House
That had no word but Stay.

Maybe, no other way
Your child could ever know
(15) Why a little House would have you stay,
When a little Road says, Go.

      —Josephine Preston Peabody, "The House and the Road"

19. Which of the following phrases best describes the narrator of the poem?
- **a.** frightened and careful
- **b.** adventuresome and carefree
- **c.** thoughtful but determined
- **d.** happy but nervous
- **e.** uncertain and critical

20. Which is the most likely explanation of "Though heart be sore for the little House" (line 11)?
- **a.** The narrator is angry at the little House.
- **b.** The narrator has mixed feelings about the little House.
- **c.** The narrator will miss the little House.
- **d.** The narrator is indifferent to the little House.
- **e.** The narrator worries about the future of the little House.

21. Which of the following best describes what the Road is compared to?
- **a.** a homesick child
- **b.** a little House
- **c.** a curious person
- **d.** the narrator's family
- **e.** a new home

22. Which of the following best describes the poem's theme?

   a. It is natural for a child to want to run away.

   b. It is natural for a child to fear the future.

   c. It is natural for a child to stay safe at home.

   d. It is natural for a child to want to leave home.

   e. It is natural for a child to miss his or her home.

23. Which of the following techniques does the poet use most in the poem?

   a. foreshadowing

   b. personification

   c. flashbacks

   d. onomatopoeia

   e. alliteration

Questions 24 through 29 refer to the following excerpt from an extended protection plan.

What Happens If It Breaks?

The Big Deal Protection Plan

2-Year Protection Plan—Extended Warranty Plan #35671

(5) This is a contract that you have purchased to protect your XZ23 computer for a period of two years. Henceforth throughout the contract you, will be referred to as "purchaser," and the Big Deal Protection Plan will be referred to as "provider." Your computer will (10) be referred to as "product." Your purchase receipt contains the effective start date of this policy and must be shown before any work is undertaken on the machine.

Coverage

(15) The plan covers parts and labor costs to repair purchaser's product should such product fail to operate correctly due to:

   ■ defect in materials

   ■ dust or condensation

(20)   ■ normal wear or tear

   ■ power surge

If provider determines that purchaser's product cannot be repaired, provider will replace it with a comparable product or (25) reimburse purchaser for replacement of the product with a voucher card equal to the current retail value of the product as determined by provider.

In addition, purchaser can expect:

(30)   ■ one battery repair or replacement when the original battery is defective as determined by provider

   ■ repair or replacement of chargers that were included in the original product

(35)   ■ one bulb replacement of purchaser's original bulb for desktop projectors

   ■ repair of image burn-in for product monitors

Exclusions

(40) The plan does not cover the following:

   ■ damage to purchaser's product caused by an accident, abuse, neglect, or intentional physical damage

   ■ products that have been lost or stolen

(45)   ■ cosmetic damage to the product, such as scratches or dents

   ■ damage to or loss of software

   ■ products with a serial number that has been altered

(50) **Service**

1. Visit bigdealprotection.com or call 1-800-BIG-DEAL to access information about service.

2. If purchaser has purchased a plan that (55) provides for home service, purchaser will need to arrange this; otherwise, purchaser may need to bring the product to a repair shop.

3. Repairs and replacements will be done at (60) provider's repair shop at provider's discretion.

4. If provider determines the product cannot be repaired, we will give purchaser a replacement within 30 days' time.

24. Based on the excerpt, which of the following will result in receiving a new computer?
   a. smoke damage due to a fire
   b. a lightning storm hitting the main drive
   c. water damage because of a hole in a roof
   d. virus destroying a word processing program
   e. dropping the computer when moving

25. Which of the following best restates the phrase "provider will replace it with a comparable product or reimburse purchaser for replacement of the product with a voucher card equal to the current retail value of the product as determined by provider" (lines 23 through 28)?
   a. The company will give the purchaser a similar computer or a credit for another computer that has the same value, which the company will figure out.
   b. The company will replace the computer with another one that may not be new but works and has been updated so that it is the same value as the original computer.
   c. The insurance company will ask the retailer to find a computer that has about the same value as the one that was sold to the purchaser.
   d. The company will give the purchaser another computer while they try to repair the broken computer, but it may not be the same make or model.
   e. The company will have its repair person assess the value of the computer and send the purchaser a check for that amount.

26. Which best describes the style in which this excerpt is written?
   a. detailed and technical
   b. dry and clinical
   c. lighthearted
   d. threatening
   e. tentative

27. Which of the following best describes how the excerpt is organized?
   a. by listing the terms of the agreement in logical order
   b. by listing parts that are covered according to their cost
   c. by listing all coverage in the order of its importance
   d. by listing what is covered first and then what is not covered
   e. by listing the various problems that could occur and how to rectify them

28. What advantage does the purchaser have by taking out the extended warranty?
   a. The machine is covered the moment the purchaser buys it.
   b. The purchaser's coverage includes replacing a machine if it is stolen.
   c. The purchaser's coverage is longer and more thorough.
   d. The machine is covered for any problem that might arise.
   e. The purchaser's coverage ensures a new machine if the first one has a problem.

29. What might possibly happen if the purchaser does not have a receipt?
   a. The warranty would not be in effect without it.
   b. An extra charge would be levied.
   c. It would complicate finding out about the coverage.
   d. It would lessen the extent of the contract.
   e. The purchaser would have to pay for repairs over a certain amount.

Questions 30 through 35 refer to the following excerpt from a novel.

Will She Marry Him?

It was Stewart Snyder whom she had always encouraged. He was so much manlier than the others; he was impressive, like his new ready-made suit with its padded shoulders.
(5) She sat with him upon a pile of presidential overshoes in the coat-closet under the stairs. As they drank two cups of coffee and nibbled at a chicken patty, the sounds of the orchestra seeped into the tiny room. Stewart
(10) whispered:

"I can't stand it, this breaking up after four years! College was the happiest time of our lives."

She believed it. "Oh, I know! To think
(15) that in just a few days we'll be parting, and we'll never see some of the bunch again!"

"Carol, you got to listen to me! You always duck when I try to talk seriously to you, but you got to listen to me. I'm going to
(20) be a big lawyer, maybe a judge, and I need you, and I'd protect you—"

His arm slid behind her shoulders. The insinuating music drained her independence. She said mournfully, "Would you take care of
(25) me?" She touched his hand. It was warm, solid.

"You bet I would! We'd have, we'd have bully times in Yankton, where I'm going to settle—"
(30) "But I want to do something with my life."

"What's better than making a comfy home and bringing up some cute kids and knowing nice, homey people?"
(35) "Of course. I know. I suppose that's so. Honestly, I do love children. But there's lots of women that can do housework, but I— well, if you have got a college education, you ought to use it for the world."
(40) "I know, but you can use it just as well in the home. And gee, Carol, just think of a bunch of us going out on a picnic some nice spring evening."

"Yes."
(45) "And sleigh-riding in winter, and going fishing—"

Blarrrrrrr! The orchestra had crashed into the "Soldiers' Chorus"; and she was protesting, "No! No! You're a dear, but I want
(50) to do things. I don't understand myself, but I want—everything in the world! Maybe I can't sing or write, but I know I can have an influence working in a library or school. Just suppose I encouraged some boy and he
(55) became a great artist! I will! I will do it! Stewart, dear, I can't settle down to nothing but dish-washing!"

After graduation she never saw Stewart Snyder again. She wrote to him once a
(60) week—for one month.

—Adapted from Sinclair Lewis, *Main Street* (1920)

30. Based on the excerpt, how would you describe Carol?
   a. fearless but needy
   b. emotional and changeable
   c. stubborn and direct
   d. demure but determined
   e. fanciful and fun

31. Based on the information in the excerpt, Stewart would most likely participate in which of the following activities?
   a. go for a ride in the country on Sunday
   b. attend a political demonstration
   c. backpack through Europe
   d. attend a seminar on ancient art
   e. play poker with the guys

32. How does the sound of the orchestra relate to the action of the scene?
   a. It helps the reader pay attention to the action.
   b. It emphasizes Carol's desire to do something with her life.
   c. It interrupts the exchange between Carol and Stewart.
   d. It mirrors Carol's strong feelings about settling down.
   e. It distracts from the ongoing action.

33. What is the most likely meaning of lines 59 and 60: "She wrote to him once a week—for one month"?
   a. It shows that their relationship was over.
   b. It shows the reader that Carol is irresponsible.
   c. It lets the reader know that Carol cared about Stewart.
   d. It emphasizes how little Carol and Stewart knew each other.
   e. It shows how fickle Carol is.

34. What effect does the fact that they are graduating have on the mood of the story?
   a. It suggests that the story is a metaphor for life.
   b. It shows how quickly life passes by.
   c. It gives the story more depth.
   d. It gives the story a sense of finality.
   e. It makes the story more exciting.

35. Which of the following is closest to the lesson the excerpt teaches?
   a. Ordinary life can be meaningful.
   b. Young people rarely know what they want.
   c. College makes individuals want to achieve great things.
   d. Individuals must find their own way.
   e. The future is always unknown.

Questions 36 through 40 refer to the following excerpt from a review.

Why Should We Clap Our Hands?

Clap your hands for *Clap Your Hands*, the new musical that opened Wednesday evening to raves from the audience. I was there for that magical evening of song and dance, and
(5)   unlike many musicals, this one even had a believable scenario.

Marty (Ellen Dayton) and Jonnie (Irving Landers) were perfectly charming as the young couple who are thrown together
(10)   by circumstances and ultimately, after a long and difficult path, become stars of a new Broadway show. This show within a show plot might seem a bit hackneyed, but not in this instance. It worked perfectly because of
(15)   the natural talent the two have, not to mention the chemistry between them. It also allowed for some of the most creative show tunes and dance routines that I have heard or seen in recent memory.

(20)   Music and lyrics by Arthur
Christianson shined, as did the choreography
by Gianno Eliano. Perhaps the only fault I
could find was the chorus's too avid
background chatter, which proved to
(25)   distract from rather than enhance the many
scenes that they were in. But a bit more
direction by Matty Guerin would solve that
problem immediately.

The writing was crisp and the dialogue
(30)   filled with witty one-liners that would blow
away even the most critical malcontent. If
you decide to see this production, you will
also witness a show that features real
ensemble work that allows the energy of the
(35)   entire cast to shine, something most casts are
not capable of doing.

Even the children were terrific. Little
Lora (Wendy Caesar) is definitely a
showstopper when she belts out "Why Me?"
(40)   to the audience without any trace of
self-consciousness.

I guess you get the idea. For those who
didn't understand: This is the best musical
I've seen in about 20 years. I give it five
(45)   stars for its energy, creativity, and wonderful
talent, something that is rare in this day of
giant productions without much thought.
Make sure to see it.

36. What does the author suggest by lines 3 and 4:
"I was there for that magical evening of song
and dance"?
   a. that many other productions are tiresome
   b. that this production is about magic
   c. that some productions do not include music
   d. that the story line for the musical was hard
   to follow
   e. that many people could not understand the
   songs' lyrics

37. Which of the following best describes the tone
of this excerpt?
   a. breezy but sobering
   b. sharp but enthusiastic
   c. humorous and direct
   d. clever but plodding
   e. fresh and thoughtful

38. Which of the following best expresses the
author's opinion of the chorus?
   a. They did not help the production.
   b. They were noisy without cause.
   c. They were bad actors.
   d. They had too many lines.
   e. They were unrehearsed.

39. Which of the following best describes the style
in which this review is written?
   a. methodical
   b. sophisticated
   c. casual
   d. technical
   e. flowery

40. Why does the author probably include the last
paragraph?
   a. to make sure the reader gets the main point
   of the review
   b. to indicate that his writing is difficult to
   understand
   c. to show that he is knowledgeable about
   musicals
   d. to emphasize why musicals are agreeable
   e. to irritate those people who did not like the
   musical

Answers

What Does Daisy Want?

1. e. While some of the choices may seem attractive, the real reason that Daisy is upset is that she wants Winterbourne to pay more attention to her. She turns on him when she thinks he is paying another woman more attention than she is receiving.

2. e. Winterbourne is definitely startled by Daisy's behavior because she changed her way of dealing with him so abruptly.

3. a. This is the best description of what is going on between Daisy and Winterbourne in the excerpt. They seem to be caring toward each other, but the scene is definitely tense.

4. e. This is clearly a priority for Daisy. The other choices are not supported by the passage. She might or might not visit his aunt. She certainly is not going to apologize, and there is no reason to believe she will leave for America or refuse to see Winterbourne again.

5. c. This is the best answer. Daisy may be a tiny bit jealous, but she definitely overreacts. She is dramatic in what she does and says.

6. a. This is the meaning of "Just at the last." The excerpt makes it clear that Winterbourne is leaving soon, but there is no mention or suggestion of him wanting her to leave, that he is breaking up with her, or that he feels bitterness toward her.

7. d. Daisy and Winterbourne are both curious about the other. This answer is supported by the excerpt in the way they want to find out about each other.

Will They Meet Again?

8. b. Nina certainly has a playful side, but she is also serious. The reader can see this by her interaction with Jim: They dance at first and laugh at the end, but in the middle section, she asks him when he ships out and whether he is frightened.

9. d. Jim does seem easygoing in his manner, and he is very appreciative of what Nina does for him. The other descriptions do not fit with how Jim is portrayed in the excerpt.

10. d. Jim and Nina have fun, but they also reveal themselves to one another. This makes the best choice *intimate*. There are lighthearted moments and serious moments, but these do not best describe the entire passage.

11. d. Based on the excerpt, Nina wants Jim to feel hope that he will return to see her after the war. This is the best answer. It is doubtful that she really thinks it will bring Jim good fortune.

12. c. This is the best choice. This is what Nina enjoys doing; the other choices are not supported by the excerpt. She doesn't seem self-centered or need to be in control. And there is nothing to suggest she studies singing, even though she seems to like to sing.

13. b. Based on the excerpt, this is the best answer. Nina would actually be just doing her job. In doing so, she might share some personal interest in the soldiers she dances with, so while choice **c** is a possibility, it is not the best answer.

Will She Land Her Jump?

14. b. This is what Yolanda learns. There is no suggestion that too much practice is detrimental, or bad, for her. She probably already knows that skating is an art form, and there is no reason to think she needs a stricter coach. She certainly practices enough.

15. d. Yolanda had to internalize doing the jump before she could do it. That is why she had her dream. Although some of the choices, like **a** and **c**, are probably true, they are not the main idea of the passage.

16. c. This answer reflects the meaning of the dream—that Yolanda could feel herself soaring through the air. It helps her master the jump.

17. a. This is how she sees herself in the dream and even after she wakes up. She does not assume she will make the jump, but only has a good feeling about it.

18. b. Based on the excerpt, the reader can determine that Yolanda is committed and receptive. This is the best description of her. While she is realistic and competitive (choice **a**), she also has a receptive quality that is central to her character.

Why Must She Go?

19. c. This is the best answer. The speaker is clearly thoughtful, but she is also determined to leave the House. She may be adventuresome, but she surely is not carefree. She is very thoughtful instead.

20. c. The line suggests that the narrator will miss the House. She doesn't really worry about its future, and she is definitely not angry with the House.

21. c. The Road is most like a curious child who wants to go out and learn things. The Road is not like a little House, the narrator's family, a new home, or a homesick child.

22. d. While it may be natural for a child to miss his home (choice **e**), this isn't the main theme of the poem. Some of the other choices might also be true in general, but they are not the main point of the poem.

23. b. While there is some alliteration in the poem, the bulk of the poem uses personification, giving human attributes to things, such as the House and the Road.

What Happens If It Breaks?

24. b. If you read the plan carefully, you will see that a power surge, such as a lightning strike, could result in receiving a new computer. The other options are not listed as being covered. None of the other choices are caused by normal wear or tear, defective materials, or dust or condensation, which are listed as covered as well.

25. a. This is a restatement of the information in the protection plan. It is the only choice that states that the company will replace the computer if necessary and explains exactly what will happen if the computer cannot be fixed.

26. a. The way in which the protection plan is written is extremely *detailed and technical* because it lists so much information about what may happen to the computer and what is covered. The style certainly isn't *lighthearted, threatening,* or *tentative,* and although it might be considered *dry,* it isn't really *clinical.*

27. d. This is the way the protection plan is organized—listing what is covered and then what is not covered. It is not organized in the manner suggested by the other choices.

28. c. The reader can figure out that the coverage for the extended plan is longer and more thorough than the normal plan that might come with the computer. The other choices might be possible, but they are not correct.

29. c. It would stand to reason that the warranty would still be valid, but it would be more complicated to access it. The other choices are not supported by the plan.

Will She Marry Him?

30. d. This choice best describes Carol. She keeps things to herself for the most part, but she is clearly determined. She doesn't seem at all needy or changeable.

31. a. It seems clear from Stewart's idea of his life that this would be most logical choice for him. Backpacking or attending a political demonstration do not seem as likely for him, and neither do playing poker or going to a seminar on ancient art.

32. d. The music acts as a reflection of the tension that Carol feels in the excerpt. It reflects her feelings about settling down with Stewart and her outburst of "No! No!"

33. a. The fact that she stopped writing after "one month" demonstrates that the relationship, like the letter writing, was over. It does not show that Carol was fickle; it is obvious that she did not want to settle down with Stewart.

34. d. There is a sense of finality because their graduation marks the end of their school years together. This is the best answer. It is not a metaphor for life, nor does it suggest how short life is.

35. d. This is the best answer. Carol had to go her own way. College may make some people want to achieve great things, but not everyone (choice **c**).

Why Should We Clap Our Hands?

36. a. The reviewer loved this musical, which is why he thought it was "magical" in the "fantastic and wonderful" sense of the word. Choice **b** uses the word *magic*, but not the way the reviewer intended. Since this play was so wonderful, it can be assumed that not all plays the reviewer sees are wonderful and that many are boring or tiresome.

37. b. This is the tone of the review. Some of the comments are *sharp*, but most of them are *enthusiastic*. The review certainly is not *sobering* or *plodding*. It might have been somewhat *humorous*, but it is not *direct*.

38. a. This is what the author means when he talks about the chorus. They were noisy, but they were supposed to be, so it was not without cause.

39. b. The review is written in a sophisticated style; the language is not simple, and the author is very knowledgeable about theater.

40. a. This is the intent of the last paragraph: to emphasize what the author's opinion is. He is re-emphasizing his main point, which was that the play should be seen by anyone remotely interested in theater.

Diagnostic Bloom Thinking Skill Analysis

The question numbers below correspond to the skill being tested

	Comprehension	Application	Analysis	Synthesis
Nonfiction	24, 36, 38	25, 28, 40	26, 27, 37, 39	29, 38, 39
Fiction	1, 2, 15, 18, 30	4, 6, 31, 32	3, 5, 14, 17, 33	7, 10, 16, 34, 35
Poetry	22	20, 21, 23	20, 21	19
Drama	9	8	11, 12	10, 13

C H A P T E R

PRACTICE TEST 2

CHAPTER SUMMARY

Here is another sample test based on the GED® Language Arts, Reading test. After working through the review in Chapters 3 through 7, take this test to see how much your score has improved from the diagnostic test in Chapter 2.

Like the diagnostic test, this practice exam mirrors the real GED® Language Arts, Reading test. It consists of 40 multiple-choice questions on reading passages. For this practice test, time yourself. On test day, you will have 65 minutes to complete this part of the exam.

The answer sheet you should use for the multiple-choice questions is on the following page. Then comes the exam itself. After that is the answer key, in which each answer is explained to help you find out why the correct answers are right and why the incorrect answers are wrong.

Practice Test 2

1. ⓐ ⓑ ⓒ ⓓ ⓔ
2. ⓐ ⓑ ⓒ ⓓ ⓔ
3. ⓐ ⓑ ⓒ ⓓ ⓔ
4. ⓐ ⓑ ⓒ ⓓ ⓔ
5. ⓐ ⓑ ⓒ ⓓ ⓔ
6. ⓐ ⓑ ⓒ ⓓ ⓔ
7. ⓐ ⓑ ⓒ ⓓ ⓔ
8. ⓐ ⓑ ⓒ ⓓ ⓔ
9. ⓐ ⓑ ⓒ ⓓ ⓔ
10. ⓐ ⓑ ⓒ ⓓ ⓔ
11. ⓐ ⓑ ⓒ ⓓ ⓔ
12. ⓐ ⓑ ⓒ ⓓ ⓔ
13. ⓐ ⓑ ⓒ ⓓ ⓔ
14. ⓐ ⓑ ⓒ ⓓ ⓔ
15. ⓐ ⓑ ⓒ ⓓ ⓔ
16. ⓐ ⓑ ⓒ ⓓ ⓔ
17. ⓐ ⓑ ⓒ ⓓ ⓔ

18. ⓐ ⓑ ⓒ ⓓ ⓔ
19. ⓐ ⓑ ⓒ ⓓ ⓔ
20. ⓐ ⓑ ⓒ ⓓ ⓔ
21. ⓐ ⓑ ⓒ ⓓ ⓔ
22. ⓐ ⓑ ⓒ ⓓ ⓔ
23. ⓐ ⓑ ⓒ ⓓ ⓔ
24. ⓐ ⓑ ⓒ ⓓ ⓔ
25. ⓐ ⓑ ⓒ ⓓ ⓔ
26. ⓐ ⓑ ⓒ ⓓ ⓔ
27. ⓐ ⓑ ⓒ ⓓ ⓔ
28. ⓐ ⓑ ⓒ ⓓ ⓔ
29. ⓐ ⓑ ⓒ ⓓ ⓔ
30. ⓐ ⓑ ⓒ ⓓ ⓔ
31. ⓐ ⓑ ⓒ ⓓ ⓔ
32. ⓐ ⓑ ⓒ ⓓ ⓔ
33. ⓐ ⓑ ⓒ ⓓ ⓔ
34. ⓐ ⓑ ⓒ ⓓ ⓔ

35. ⓐ ⓑ ⓒ ⓓ ⓔ
36. ⓐ ⓑ ⓒ ⓓ ⓔ
37. ⓐ ⓑ ⓒ ⓓ ⓔ
38. ⓐ ⓑ ⓒ ⓓ ⓔ
39. ⓐ ⓑ ⓒ ⓓ ⓔ
40. ⓐ ⓑ ⓒ ⓓ ⓔ
41. ⓐ ⓑ ⓒ ⓓ ⓔ
42. ⓐ ⓑ ⓒ ⓓ ⓔ
43. ⓐ ⓑ ⓒ ⓓ ⓔ
44. ⓐ ⓑ ⓒ ⓓ ⓔ
45. ⓐ ⓑ ⓒ ⓓ ⓔ
46. ⓐ ⓑ ⓒ ⓓ ⓔ
47. ⓐ ⓑ ⓒ ⓓ ⓔ
48. ⓐ ⓑ ⓒ ⓓ ⓔ
49. ⓐ ⓑ ⓒ ⓓ ⓔ
50. ⓐ ⓑ ⓒ ⓓ ⓔ

Directions: Choose the *one best answer* to each question.

Questions 1 through 7 refer to the following excerpt from a novel.

Will She Let Him Help Her?

"My goodness—you can't go on living here!" Rosedale exclaimed.

Lily smiled. "I am not sure that I can,
(5) either; but I have gone over my expenses
very carefully, and I rather think I shall be
able to manage it."

"Be able to manage it? That's not what
I mean—it's no place for you!"

"It's what I mean. I have been out of
(10) work for the last week."

"Out of work—out of work! What a
way for you to talk! The idea of your having
to work—it's preposterous." He brought out
his sentences in short violent jerks, as though
(15) they were forced up from a deep inner crater
of indignation. "It's a farce—a crazy farce,"
he repeated, his eyes fixed on the long vista
of the room reflected in the glass between
the windows.

(20) Lily continued to meet his arguments
with a smile. "I don't know why I should
regard myself as an exception—" she began.

"Because you *are*; that's why. And your
being in a place like this is an outrage. I can't
(25) talk of it calmly."

She had in truth never seen him so
shaken out of his usual glibness. There was
something almost moving to her in his
inarticulate struggle with his emotions.

(30) He rose with a start, which left the
rocking chair quivering on its beam ends,
and placed himself squarely before her.

"Look here, Miss Lily, I'm going to
Europe next week: going over to Paris and
(35) London for a couple of months—and I can't
leave you like this. I can't do it. I know it's
none of my business—you've let me
understand that often enough—but things
are worse with you now than they have been
(40) before, and you must see that you've got to
accept help from somebody. You spoke to me
the other day about some debt to Trenor. I
know what you mean—and I respect you for
feeling as you do about it."

(45) A blush of surprise rose to Lily's pale
face, but before she could interrupt him, he
had continued eagerly: "Well, I'll lend you
the money to pay Trenor; and I won't—I—
see here, don't take me up till I've finished.
(50) What I mean is, it'll be a plain business
arrangement, such as one man would make
with another. Now, what have you got to say
against that?"

—Adapted from Edith Wharton,
The House of Mirth

1. Why is Rosedale upset?
   a. Lily is out of work and cannot pay her rent.
   b. Lily is living in a place he thinks is beneath her.
   c. Lily will not accept him as a suitor.
   d. Lily will not do what he wants her to do.
   e. Lily is physically and emotionally unwell.

2. How does Lily react to what Rosedale says?
   a. She is impressed but also embarrassed.
   b. She thinks he is much too forward.
   c. She is worried the arrangement will not work out.
   d. She believes that he is dangerous.
   e. She would like him to leave at once.

3. Based on the excerpt, what can the reader infer about Lily?

   a. She is afraid of her future.

   b. She has no educational background.

   c. She is needy and requires others' kindnesses.

   d. She is very proud and independent.

   e. She has little emotion.

4. Which of the following best explains why Rosedale says that Lily's being out of work is "a farce"?

   a. He believes she should not have to work.

   b. He thinks that no women should work.

   c. He believes she made the job up.

   d. He wants to marry her.

   e. He thinks she is too old to work.

5. Based on the excerpt, which best describes Rosedale?

   a. rude and self-involved

   b. blunt and determined

   c. cautious and mannered

   d. emotional but retiring

   e. sympathetic but shy

6. What is the mood of the excerpt?

   a. carefree

   b. romantic

   c. depressed

   d. frantic

   e. intense

7. What is implied about the relationship between Lily and Rosedale in the past?

   a. She was unaware that he cared about her.

   b. She was not interested in him as a suitor.

   c. She hardly knew him at all until recently.

   d. She liked him but thought he did not care for her.

   e. She worried that he was too self-absorbed.

Questions 8 through 13 refer to the following excerpt from a play.

Will They Do Something Spontaneous?

[A couple is walking along a city street, and as they walk, they talk.]

Lucy: I love James Dean, don't you, Barry?

(5) Barry: Oh, he's okay, I guess, if you like that type.

Lucy: What's wrong with his type?

Barry: Well, he comes on like a rebel, against any kind of social setup. He's like a beatnik.

Lucy: You mean like Jack Kerouac?

(10) Barry: Well, not exactly. Kerouac has some kind of message. It may not be to my liking, but he's got a real philosophy. Dean may be rebellious, but it seems a bit staged to me.

Lucy: Really? I think he's a divine actor.
(15) What's wrong with being rebellious? You could use a bit of rebellion yourself. You're such a stick-in-the-mud. Work, work, work. Responsibility, responsibility, responsibility. Don't you ever want to do something on the
(20) spur of the moment? Be a little bit wild? Why don't we do something wild? Let's take off tomorrow for a few days and go somewhere exotic. Just tell them that your mother is sick. They'll understand. They'll let you go for a
(25) few days. We could be like beatniks! It would be fun.

Barry: I can't do that, Lucy. You know there's far too much work to do. I can't just take off. What would happen to all my cases?
(30) I'm due in court all next week.

Lucy: Well, then, you leave me no choice. I will just have to dream about James Dean. I'm sure he would take some time off to be with me. Yes, definitely. [laughing] You're
(35) jealous, aren't you?

Barry: Me, jealous of James Dean? Ha! Absolutely not, my dear. He's on the screen, and I'm the one who's here with you, traditionalist or not. [Barry gives Lucy a
(40) quick kiss.] Let's go see that new Doris Day movie tomorrow night. I hear it's great. Now there's a good actress.

Lucy: If you say so. Sure, handsome, we can go.

8. Which of the following phrases best describes Lucy?
 a. playful and lighthearted
 b. hurtful and opinionated
 c. subdued and contented
 d. ambivalent and testy
 e. aggressive and determined

9. Based on the selection, how would Barry most likely behave if he were not a lawyer?
 a. He would become more casual.
 b. He would still be disciplined.
 c. He would take longer vacations.
 d. He would adopt a carefree life.
 e. He would become bitter.

10. How does Barry differentiate between Jack Kerouac and James Dean?
 a. He thinks Kerouac is a great man and that Dean is a modest actor.
 b. He thinks Kerouac is sincere and that Dean is a fake.
 c. He believes Kerouac has a strong sense of humor but that Dean does not.
 d. He believes Kerouac is a poor writer but that Dean is a good actor.
 e. He thinks Kerouac is too carefree and that Dean is a committed actor.

11. Which of the following best describes the mood of this scene?
 a. mostly carefree but with some serious undertones
 b. somewhat intense but not threatening
 c. easygoing and harmonious
 d. somewhat sad but with light moments
 e. mysterious and intriguing

12. Based on the excerpt, what can be inferred about Lucy's relationship with Barry?
 a. She loves to tease him.
 b. She thinks he is unapproachable.
 c. She thinks he is foolish.
 d. She finds it hard to care about him.
 e. She wants to make him uncomfortable.

13. Based on the excerpt, which of the following is Lucy probably going to do next?
 a. She will write a letter to James Dean.
 b. She will break up with Barry.
 c. She will continue to see James Dean movies.
 d. She will stop caring about James Dean.
 e. She will take a holiday by herself.

Questions 14 through 18 refer to the following excerpt from a novel.

Why Does She Want to Go?

The voice seemed to come from the dark shadows at the end of the garden. The singer sang slowly, his voice lingering caressingly on the words. The last verse died away softly
(5) and clearly, almost imperceptibly fading into silence.

For a moment, there was utter stillness, then Diana lay back with a little sigh. "The Kashmiri Song. It makes me think of India. I
(10) heard a man sing it in Kashmir last year, but not like that. What a wonderful voice!"

Arbuth looked at her curiously, surprised at the sudden ring of interest in her tone and the animation of her face.

(15) "You say you have no emotion in your nature, and yet that unknown man's singing has stirred you deeply. How do you reconcile the two?" he asked, almost angrily.

(20) "Is an appreciation of the beautiful emotion?" she challenged, with uplifted eyes. "Surely not. Music, art, nature, everything beautiful appeals to me. But there is nothing emotional in that. It is only that I prefer beautiful things to ugly ones. For that reason,

(25) even pretty clothes appeal to me," she added, laughing.

"You are the best-dressed woman in Biskra," he noted. "But is not that a concession to the womanly feelings that you

(30) despise?"

"Not at all. To take an interest in one's clothes is not an exclusively feminine vice. I like pretty dresses. I admit to spending some time in thinking of color schemes to go with

(35) my horrible hair, but I assure you that my dressmaker has an easier life than my brother's tailor."

She sat silent, hoping that the singer might not have gone, but there was no sound

(40) except a cicada chirping near her. She swung round in her chair, looking in the direction from which it came. "Listen to him. Jolly little chap! They are the first things I listen for when I get to Port Said. They mean the

(45) East to me."

"Maddening little beasts!" said Arbuth irritably.

"They are going to be very friendly little beasts to me during the next four

(50) weeks. . . . You don't know what this trip means to me. I like wild places. The happiest times of my life have been spent camping in America and India, and I have always wanted

the desert more than either of them. It is
(55) going to be a month of pure joy. I am going to be enormously happy."

—Adapted from Edith Hull, *The Sheik* (1921)

14. In what way is Diana's response to the song similar to her response to the sound of the cicada?
  a. She is unfamiliar with both of them.
  b. She thinks their sounds are similar.
  c. They remind her of faraway places.
  d. They suggest that life is comfortable.
  e. They bring up frightening emotions.

15. What is the mood of the passage?
  a. reflective
  b. troubled
  c. quarrelsome
  d. sorrowful
  e. deliberate

16. Based on the information in the passage, which of the following pairs of words best describes Diana?
  a. independent and passionate
  b. reckless and thoughtless
  c. taunting and hurtful
  d. considerate and helpful
  e. selfish and unfeeling

17. Why does Arbuth react angrily to what Diana says about the music?
  a. He thinks she is a difficult woman.
  b. He believes she is very feminine.
  c. He wants her to give up her plans.
  d. He thinks he may be in love with her.
  e. He believes that she is lying about herself.

18. Based on what is known about Diana, what is the most likely reason for her traveling to the desert?
   a. for business
   b. on a whim
   c. to meet her husband
   d. to fulfill a promise
   e. as a well-deserved vacation

Questions 19 through 23 refer to the following poem.

Why Does He Look at the Stars?

When I heard the learn'd astronomer,
When the proofs, the figures, were ranged in
   columns before me;
When I was shown the charts and the diagrams,
   to add, divide, and measure them;
When I, sitting, heard the astronomer, where he
   lectured with much applause in the
   lecture-room;
(5)   How soon, unaccountable, I became tired and
   sick,
Till rising and gliding out, I wander'd off by
   myself,
In the mystical moist night-air, and from time
   to time,
Look'd up in perfect silence at the stars.

—From Walt Whitman, "When I Heard the
Learn'd Astronomer"

19. Which best describes the poet's viewpoint of the astronomer?
   a. He knows a great deal but is uninspiring.
   b. He is a good speaker with a large following.
   c. He is ignorant about the beauty of the stars.
   d. The audience is polite but does not enjoy his speech.
   e. The audience thinks he is a genius.

20. What is the poet most likely talking about when he says, "the charts and the diagrams, to add, divide, and measure them" (line 3)?
   a. bills that he needs to pay
   b. the study of mathematics
   c. facts having to do with astronomy
   d. his budget
   e. the salaries astronomers are paid

21. Which of the following can be inferred about the poet?
   a. He enjoys learning about many subjects.
   b. He prefers experiencing things firsthand.
   c. He is not good at numbers.
   d. He knows very little about astronomy.
   e. He is very impatient.

22. Which best describes the rhyme scheme of the poem?
   a. ABCD
   b. AABB
   c. ABAB
   d. ABCB
   e. ABBA

23. Which of the following is implied by the poem?
   a. Mman has no place in nature.
   b. Book knowledge is necessary.
   c. Nature is full of wonder.
   d. Life is full of difficulties.
   e. Astronomy is a complex subject.

Questions 24 through 29 refer to the following excerpt from a company handbook.

How Will This Program Help You?

Here at Coralis, we consider our employees
like a family, and to that point we are
instituting a new program that will help
employees improve their health by staying
(5)   fit. We are in the process of creating a 3,000
square-foot, on-site gym in Building G that

will offer classes in yoga and mat Pilates as well as workout equipment and personal trainers. The facility can be utilized before, (10) after, and even during employee work hours.

After exhaustive research, our Health and Fitness Committee agreed that a company gym would offer the best option for our employees who may find it hard to fit (15) in a workout schedule when they have such a busy load of work to accomplish each day. This gym will replace our arrangement with the Fitness Today facility, which employees were encouraged to use in the past. Use of (20) the gym, as well as classes, is included as part of each employee's salary. To start, classes will be given at 8 a.m., 12 noon, and 5 p.m. General workout is available throughout the day. Personal trainers will be paid by both (25) the company and individuals, with employees paying half of the cost.

In addition to the facility, there will be an incentive program for taking part in gym activities. Each workout session will result in (30) the employee receiving a token. Accumulated tokens can be redeemed at the company cafeteria. Of course, the kind of foods that they can be redeemed for will be "heart healthy" choices such as salads, low-fat (35) meals, fruits, and vegetables. Other items may be purchased with cash.

We feel that the institution of this stellar program will go far to improve the fitness of each employee. This will doubtless (40) have a positive impact on employee production. We will also be hosting goal programs, such as weight loss and strength training initiatives. We look forward to your input about the new gym and its associated (45) activities. We at Coralis like to be first in proactive ways to keep our employees not only fit, but also happy.

24. Based on the excerpt, what can be inferred about the management of Coralis?
   a. They believe the program will improve the amount of work each employee produces.
   b. They believe the program will benefit the company by making employees less competitive.
   c. They believe the exercise program will make employees work longer hours.
   d. They believe the program will keep employees from asking for raises so frequently.
   e. They believe the program will make employees more confident.

25. Which of the following would the new exercise program most likely help?
   a. a person who has trouble staying on a diet
   b. a person who has difficulty concentrating
   c. a person going through a personal crisis
   d. a person who enjoys competitive sports
   e. a person who is having problems with meeting goals

26. Who is most likely to use a personal trainer?
   a. a temporary worker
   b. a clerk in the mailroom
   c. a salesperson who travels a lot
   d. an executive who works odd hours
   e. a person who likes classroom settings

27. Based on the excerpt, what does the token incentive system most likely have as a goal?
   a. to have people save money
   b. to expose people to healthy food
   c. to get people to exercise frequently
   d. to require people to eat healthy food
   e. to teach people how to avoid heart problems

28. What do the administrators at Coralis assume?
a. that people who exercise eat better
b. that people who exercise do better work
c. that people who exercise follow orders
d. that people who exercise are happier
e. that people who exercise lose weight

29. What is probably a major factor that led company administrators to decide to build their own gym rather than using an outside one?
a. The company gym will have more classes than the private gym.
b. The company gym will have more facilities than the private gym.
c. The company gym will be less expensive for the company in the long run.
d. The company gym will be larger than the private gym.
e. The company gym will have private trainers.

Questions 30 through 35 refer to the following excerpt from a short story.

What Will He Do?

"Nothing's going right . . . absolutely nothing," Jim said under his breath as he looked at his car. It was the third time this week it wouldn't start, which meant he
(5) would be late to work again. His troubles didn't end there, though. His girlfriend had just broken up with him, and he hadn't slept all night.

His father could see him from the
(10) living room window. He thought his son's face looked like a dried prune, it was so twisted up with anger. He felt sorry for his son. He remembered how hard it had been for him when he was just out of school and
(15) felt lost, but he didn't know how to help.

Jim walked through the door. "Hey, Dad, can you give me a ride to work? I can't get the car started—again." His father nodded and grabbed his keys.

(20) In the car there wasn't a lot of talk, until Jim mentioned he had been to the recruiting office.

"I don't want you to go into the army," his father exploded. "You don't know what it
(25) will be like. Things will start to get better. Just give yourself some time."

"There really isn't anything here for me. I need a change. I think the army would help me. Teach me some skills. I could go to
(30) college afterward."

"And what if there is no afterward? What about that? We love you, Jim. We don't want to lose you."

"That's just the chance I would have to
(35) take." Jim was aware of how his parents felt. But he wanted to do something with his life. He didn't want to wait for something to happen. He hadn't gotten into the school he wanted to attend. His girlfriend was gone.
(40) What reason was there for him to stay?

Jim took a deep breath and then started to talk in a firm tone.

"Sorry, Dad, but I've already made my decision. I signed up last week. I'm going to
(45) be leaving for training in about two weeks."

Quite suddenly, his father pulled off the road. "Jim, Jim, you did this without talking to us. Why? Why? Your mother. . . ." and his voice trailed off. He looked down. He
(50) didn't know what to do. Then he turned to his son.

"We love you, Jim," he said as he hugged him.

"I love you too, Dad. It will be all right.
(55) I promise."

30. When does the scene in this excerpt take place?
  a. late afternoon
  b. morning
  c. midday
  d. early evening
  e. just after lunch

31. Based on the information in this excerpt, how do Jim and his father's viewpoints differ?
  a. Jim feels his father is unreasonable, but his father feels that Jim is being irresponsible.
  b. Jim feels slighted by his father, and his father is bewildered by him.
  c. Jim thinks he is being realistic, and his father thinks he is rushing his decision.
  d. Jim believes his father is too idealistic, and his father feels that Jim is too opportunistic.
  e. Jim cannot relate to his father at all, while his father understands Jim's plight.

32. What form of figurative language does the author use when he or she says, "He thought his son's face looked like a dried prune, it was so twisted up with anger (lines 10 through 12)"?
  a. metaphor
  b. hyperbole
  c. simile
  d. personification
  e. alliteration

33. What is Jim's father's greatest fear?
  a. that Jim will do poorly in the military
  b. that Jim might be killed in action
  c. that Jim won't go to college
  d. that Jim will disappoint his mother
  e. that Jim may never straighten out

34. What does Jim's father suggest about how Jim's mother will react to the news that Jim has enlisted?
  a. She will be horrified by his decision.
  b. She will disown him if he leaves.
  c. She will try to take him out of the country.
  d. She will understand his predicament.
  e. She will ask the army to release him from his duty.

35. Based on the excerpt, which of the following words would the narrator most likely use to describe Jim?
  a. confused and impractical
  b. angry and spiteful
  c. cruel and determined
  d. desperate and decisive
  e. unsure and dependent

Questions 36 through 40 refer to the following excerpt from a review.

Will He Continue to Watch the Show?
Readers, I want you to know that I am not prejudiced against women, but I can't ignore the blatant, self-serving attitude of this new television series *Housewives Revealed*. Who

(5) cares what these women do? Who wants to know about their catty, little minds?

Well, apparently almost everyone does because despite my dire predictions in last month's column, *Housewives Revealed* is

(10) a smash hit, not just with middle-aged women, which might be expected, but also with the younger set and even, heaven forbid, some guys. Go figure! For me, the only reason to watch the show is to see how

(15) low these women are willing to stoop for a bit of glory—five minutes of fame. No one's going to get any acting awards, but there will be lots of publicity. And, who knows what else it will garner?

PRACTICE TEST 2

(20)   The plot of the series is, simply put, loose. In fact, there is no plot of any consequence, just endless comments and nitpicking among the team of four women who pretend they can act. Well, they do act

(25) and react, all in their own way, which varies little from who they actually are. The acting is something of a joke.

     The tryouts for the coveted roles were months in the making, with a huge number

(30) of ladies seeking the prize of a part in this new production, a cross between a sitcom and reality TV. Every Tuesday night, we are allowed into the insane, little world where there is no such thing as morality or mental

(35) courage. But so much for my ranting.

     It is a show that people want to watch. The impression is that viewers are peeking through a window watching the antics of these housewives who give such personal

(40) glimpses into their lives that one almost feels guilty. I guess that is its appeal. So enjoy it if you wish, but I hope that someday some new series—that refresh instead of embarrass— will appear on the television networks'

(45) schedules.

36. Which of the following best expresses the opinion of the author of the excerpt?
   a. The author does not feel the show should have been put on the air.
   b. The author believes that younger women will watch the show.
   c. The author feels that better actors should have been chosen for the show.
   d. The author is not sure that sitcoms are worth watching.
   e. The author dislikes the show but realizes that a lot of people like it.

37. Which of the following best describes the style in which the excerpt is written?
   a. lighthearted
   b. ill-tempered
   c. quiet
   d. inquisitive
   e. sentimental

38. Based on the information in the excerpt, which is the best description of *Housewives Revealed*?
   a. silly and joking
   b. indecent and improvised
   c. contained and structured
   d. sincere and meaningful
   e. honest and thoughtful

39. Based on the information in the excerpt, what audience is most likely to enjoy the television show?
   a. middle-aged men who are happily married
   b. women who are in difficult relationships
   c. women with young children
   d. grandparents
   e. stepparents

40. Which of the following changes would most likely cause the reviewer to have a more favorable opinion of the television show?
   a. a well-written script
   b. more female actors
   c. a plot that ends happily
   d. more of a reality show
   e. more honesty

Answers

Will She Let Him Help Her?

1. b. Rosedale clearly states that her apartment is no place for her. There is no mention of him being a suitor or that Lily is not well.

2. a. Lily is both embarrassed and impressed by Rosedale's words. She has never seen him act like this, and she blushes.

3. d. The reader should infer that Lily is headstrong; she is proud and independent. No mention is made of her education, and she can't be considered needy.

4. a. Rosedale clearly states that the idea of Lily's working is outrageous. He feels she is above having to work. His actions indicate how emotional he is about this.

5. b. Rosedale's words and his manner of speaking both point to a sense of bluntness and determination in his dealing with Lily. He is certainly not acting like a shy man.

6. e. Rosedale cannot talk calmly; the tone of the passage is indeed quite intense, and Lily has never seen him like this before. This is the best description of the excerpt's mood.

7. b. The passage suggests that Lily did not want to have Rosedale pursue her when Rosedale says, "I know it's none of my business—you've let me understand that often enough."

Will They Do Something Spontaneous?

8. a. Lucy clearly is acting playfully with her friend Barry. She teases him by saying they should run off on the spur of the moment for a few days although she knows that Barry will say no.

9. b. Even if he were not a lawyer, Barry would likely still be responsible and disciplined. It is his true nature. He is not likely to become more casual or be bitter.

10. b. Barry feels that Kerouac has a real philosophy of life, even though it is not his philosophy, while he thinks James Dean's rebellious nature is "staged." He doesn't necessarily think that Kerouac is a great man, either.

11. a. Lucy sets the mood; she is carefree and playful with Barry, but behind that façade, one senses that there are some serious overtones. The scene does not seem intense or harmonious, nor does it seem mysterious.

12. a. Lucy seems to really enjoy teasing Barry and likes playing the opposite to his seriousness because she cares about him. Although she teases him a lot, it is doubtful that she thinks he is foolish.

13. c. The passage suggests that Lucy will still go to see James Dean movies because she thinks he is a great actor. There is no suggestion that she is going to break up with Barry or take a vacation by herself.

Why Does She Want to Go?

14. c. The song reminds Diana of faraway places like Kashmir, and the cicadas are the first things she listens for when she comes to Port Said, so they both suggest faraway places. They certainly do not bring up frightening emotions, and there is nothing in the text to suggest the other possibilities, either.

15. a. The mood is reflective as Diana remembers past travels and talks about beauty and color. There is no sorrow in her thoughts. She doesn't seem quarrelsome, either.

16. a. Diana is passionate about music, art, and beautiful clothes, and she shows her independence when she challenges Arbuth with uplifted eyes.

17. e. Arbuth questions Diana about what she has said about herself—that she is not emotional—when he believes she is being emotional about the song. There is no indication that he is in love with her. He may think she is very feminine, but this isn't said in the excerpt. He doesn't appear to think she is a difficult woman, either.

18. b. Diana is presented as a person of some wealth who travels a great deal and enjoys being in wild places; she looks forward to being in the desert.

Why Does He Look at the Stars?

19. a. The astronomer lectures well and is knowledgeable, but he is not inspiring to the poet. The astronomer may or may not appreciate the beauty of the stars; the poem does not really say.

20. c. This is the best answer. The poet is talking about the technical details and facts involved in the study of astronomy. There is no mention of money, bills, or budgets.

21. b. The poet does not want to stay at the lecture about astronomy. He prefers to be alone in the night, gazing up at the stars. He enjoys experiencing things firsthand.

22. a. There is no rhyme scheme in this poem, so this is the correct answer. The other choices show internal rhyme schemes that are not present in the poem.

23. c. Although the poet agrees that the astronomer has mastered the technical details of the science of astronomy, he portrays nature as mystical. To the poet, nature will always holds surprises, and people who try to classify it and place it within a textbook are missing its real beauty.

How Will This Program Help You?

24. a. Coralis feels that the program will result in an increase in employee production because fit employees will work better. This can be seen in lines 39 through 41, where the text states that improving employee fitness "will doubtless have a positive impact on employee production."

25. a. The program will help those who have trouble staying on a diet by rewarding them with tokens that can be used for low-fat meals, fruits, and vegetables.

26. d. An executive who works odd hours would probably benefit the most since he or she probably can't attend the regularly scheduled exercise classes. A salesperson who travels a lot will not be around that much, so he or she might not be available for personal training, although it might be argued that when the salesperson is around, he or she might opt for personal training. Even so, choice **d** is the better answer.

27. b. The use of tokens will allow people to try foods for free that they might not choose otherwise. That may or may not make them healthier, too, but that is not necessarily the main goal of the program.

28. b. The assumption of the administration is that fit employees will work harder and be more productive because they will feel better and have more energy.

29. c. Outsourcing exercise facilities will probably cost more over time than having a gym on-site. So this is the best answer. The other choices are not supported by the text.

What Will He Do?

30. b. The excerpt says that Jim needed to get to work and that he did not sleep the night before. This supports the answer that the scene takes place in the morning.

31. **c.** By what happens in the scene, the reader can figure out that Jim is determined to make his own decisions, while his father would prefer it if Jim thought about it for a while.

32. **c.** The author is using a simile. The use of the word *like* indicates this. The son's face was contorted with anger, which reminded the father of the image of a dried prune.

33. **b.** Jim's father does not want to lose his son; he could be killed in action. There is no reason to believe the father fears Jim will not straighten his life out.

34. **a.** The mother will be horrified by Jim's decision to enter the army, but there is nothing in the text to support the idea that she would disown him. Her horror that he might be killed illustrates her affection for her son.

35. **d.** Jim is desperate because his girlfriend left him, and he is decisive in his choice to join the army, which he thinks will give him a new start in life.

Will He Continue to Watch the Show?

36. **e.** The author does not like the show but accepts the realty that it is a hit show that people want to watch. The other choices are not supported by the review.

37. **b.** The author's tone is quite ill-tempered and not tolerant at all of the television series. There is nothing sentimental or lighthearted about it.

38. **b.** The author believes that viewing people's regular lives is like peering into someone's window, which is indecent and inappropriate. Because there is no real script, all dialogue is improvised in the sense that the women decide what they are going to say as events happen. The author is not saying that the show is honest or meaningful.

39. **b.** Women who are in difficult relationships will most likely be drawn to this show because it will offer them some respite to see actors nit-picking on TV.

40. **a.** The author would appreciate a well-written script rather than a show that is basically scriptless. This is the best answer.

Diagnostic Bloom Thinking Skill Analysis

The question numbers below correspond to the skill being tested

	Comprehension	Application	Analysis	Synthesis
Nonfiction	25, 36, 38	26, 29, 39	24, 27, 37	28, 40
Fiction	1, 2, 16, 30	4, 33	5, 7, 14, 17, 31, 34	3, 6, 15, 32, 35
Poetry	20	22	19	21, 23
Drama	8	9, 13	10, 12	11

ADITIONAL ONLINE PRACTICE ▶

Whether you need help building basic skills or preparing for an exam, visit LearningExpress Practice Center! Using the code below, you'll be able to access additional online practice. This online practice will also provide you with:

Immediate scoring
Detailed answer explanations
A customized diagnostic report that will assess your skills and focus your study

Log into the LearningExpress Practice Center by using the URL: **www.learnatest.com/practice**

This is your Access Code: **7953**

Follow the steps online to redeem your access code. After you've used your access code to register with the site, you will be prompted to create a username and password. For easy reference, record them here:

Username: _Hilliard 100_   **Password:** _library_

If you have any questions or problems, please contact LearningExpress customer service at 1-800-295-9556 ext. 2, or e-mail us at **customerservice@learningexpressllc.com**